Sleep On It

Prepare Delicious Meals the Night Before That You Can Pop in the Oven the Next Day!

Carol Gordon

HYPERION

New York

LIBRARY OF CONGRESS CATALOGING-IN-PUBLICATION DATA

Gordon, Carol
Sleep on it : prepare delicious meals the night before that you can pop in the oven the next day! / Carol Gordon.—1st ed.
p.   cm.
Includes index.
ISBN 1-4013-0816-3
1. Make-ahead cookery.   I. Title.

TX652.G667   2005
641.5'55—dc22
2005050352

Hyperion books are available for special promotions and premiums. For details contact Michael Rentas, Assistant Director, Inventory Operations, Hyperion, 77 West 66th Street, 11th floor, New York, New York 10023, or call 212-456-0133.

Book design by Richard Oriolo

FIRST EDITION

10   9   8   7   6   5   4   3   2   1

To Jennifer and Erik

my joy, my sunshine, my

most wonderful gift!

Contents

Acknowledgments

Sincere gratitude to my agent, Meredith Bernstein, who trusted her instincts, came on board, and guided me through the birthing process of *Sleep On It*. To my editor, Leslie Wells, for her infinite patience with a first-time author and her encouragement every step of the way. And to Denise Landis, who tested all the recipes, fed the multitudes, and gave me invaluable feedback.

Many thanks to the friends and family members who shared their favorite recipes with me for this book:

Ellen Kirkpatrick, Durango, CO: Bayou Bend Casserole, Ellie's Sunday Strata
Katherine Mikkelson, Arlington Heights, IL: Hattie's Eggs, Holiday Yeast Rolls
Stephanie Morse, Indianapolis, IN: Spicy Sausage Meatballs, Maggi's Famous Blue Cheese Ball, Chocolate Chip Oatmeal Cookies
Gail Tilton, Chatham, MA: Artichoke Spinach Dip
Courtney Blankenship, Orleans, MA: Super Bowl Meatballs, Mushroom Rolls
Julie Widrow, Stoughton, MA: Nantucket House Upside-Down French Toast, The Most Amazing Brisket Ever

Jane Sullivan, Germantown, MD: Shrimp Rémoulade

Jennifer Maulfair, Round Hill, VA: Chili Cheese Puff

Barbara Zittel, Latham, NY: Vidalia Onion Corn
Casserole

Gigi Gerstle, Chatham, MA: Eggplant Mozzarella

Nancy Petrus, Chatham, MA: Mushroom Celebration,
Never-Fail Hash Browns

Patricia Marini, Chatham, MA: Eggplant Parma Style

Sandra Brittain, Towson, MD: Monte Cristo
Sandwiches

Michelle Kleinkauf, Chicago, IL: Salmon Mexicana

Alek Komarnitsky, Lafayette, CO: Sweet Honey BBQ
Shrimp, Spicy BBQ Shrimp

Bill and Susan Mosca, Lovell, ME: Margaret Mosca's
Zuppa Inglese (Italian Rum Cake)

Carol Brezovec, Westport, CT: Chocolate Mousse
Crown

Kelly and Bobby Kennedy, West Hartford, CT: Kelly's
Cheese Spread, Walnut Carrot Raisin Muffins

Gail Clark, Darnestown, MD: Karen's Chuck Steak, Veal
with Peppers and Mushrooms

Jim Metzger, Chester, VA: King Ranch Turkey

Jane Drew, Chatham, MA: Marinated Vegetable Salad,
Potluck Casserole

Justin Rivers, Chatham, MA: Pork Loin Extraordinaire

Claudia Shepardson, South Yarmouth, MA: Salsa-
Marinated Chicken with Spiced Orange Butter, Piña
Colada Tiramisù

Kathy Ellis, Darnestown, MD: Buster Bar Dessert

Lillian Garnett, Chatham, MA: Chocolate-Covered
Peanut Butter Balls

Mary Chestnut, Chatham, MA: Frothy Strawberry
    Squares
Andrew Schloss, Elkins Park, PA, Food writer: Apple,
    Blue Cheese, and Bacon Cheesecake, Brandy
    Cheesecake
Erik Oblinger, Framingham, MA: Sunday Night Supper
Marilyn Jensen, Chatham, MA: Crabmeat Canapés
Ellen English, Roseland, VA, Chef: Virginia Ham Tarts

To my friends behind the scenes—thanks for your help
and encouragement:

Amy Andreasson and the staff at the Eldredge Library
Mary Sherman and Donald Howes—their spirit lives on
Stephanie Morse, for her support and lifetime friendship
Priscilla Painton, the busiest person I know, who took
    time to proof and comment on my draft, galleys, and
    so forth—thanks for your friendship
Sandra Brittain, my buddy of thirty-seven years, thanks
    for packing your bags and sharing our New York
    adventure
Judy Llewellyn, your friendship and guidance with this
    new endeavor meant so much
Annie Stewart, for spending long, long hours
    proofreading the manuscript
Anne Le Claire, for mentoring me from the very
    conception of *Sleep On It*
Jacky Generous, for the laughs and ideas we shared
    during our walks
Jill Meyer, for her endless on-the-spot computer help
Diane Lampke, for her tireless energy in helping to wrap
    up this manuscript

My family is always first in my heart. I couldn't have reached this amazing time in my life without your love and support: Jennifer, Jim, Ella, Beatrice, Erik, Jackie, and the Joseph Newman family. To Jerry, my husband, my rock: Thanks for keeping me centered, restoring my sanity, and catering to my every whim during this process! And, to my mother-in-law, Carole La Roche, who made our innkeeping experience possible.

To all the guests who have graced our doorstep at the Nantucket House of Chatham Bed and Breakfast, thanks for giving us the experience of a lifetime!

"To cook is to share the love of family and friends."

Introduction

 Sand in your shoes, walking in the steps of Thoreau, the breeze off Nantucket Sound on a summer's night, the ever-changing sea, the Chatham fog—that's the Cape Cod we love.

Chatham is a fascinating mix of past and present. The historic Nantucket House of Chatham Bed and Breakfast is believed to have been built for a sea captain circa 1804 on the island of Nantucket. When the prosperous whaling industry began to fail, the house was floated over to its present South Chatham location in 1867.

My husband, Jerry, and I bought the Nantucket House of Chatham on May 26, 1999, and began our innkeeping adventure. Little did we know what was in store for us! We had two weeks until our first full house of guests were to arrive for a family reunion. A call to our friends and family had everyone front and center to help us through a grueling two weeks. Finally, we were ready. June 10 brought our first guests. Everyone was excited.

My first innkeeping morning found me in the kitchen cutting fruit at 4:30 A.M.! Right then and there, I knew if we were going to remain in this business, I needed to find some time-saving shortcuts. I began coveting overnight recipes and, finding them few and far between, the concept of *Sleep On It* was born. As an innkeeper, I know what it's like to grab a moment whenever I can. *Sleep On It* is my ultimate time-saver. This compilation of overnight recipes allows you to serve a delicious breakfast, brunch, dinner, or dessert and still have time to enjoy your day doing whatever makes you happy. Like me, you'll value the convenience these recipes bring into your life. I love my beach naps!

Whether you've just learned to cook or have been cooking all your life, you'll enjoy *Sleep On It*, this special collection of recipes from other inns as well as favorites from family and friends. You'll also get a laugh as innkeepers share their innkeeping experiences.

From breakfast through dinner and dessert—we've got it covered. Carpe diem!

Carol Gordon
Nantucket House of Chatham Bed and Breakfast
www.chathaminn.com
www.overnightrecipes.com

NOTE: Most health departments now advise against
using raw eggs in overnight recipes. Be sure to
use pasteurized eggs in overnight recipes
that call for uncooked eggs.

Appetizers

Appetizers used to be my least favorite things to make. Then along came the scrumptious Mushroom Rolls on page 28. They're perfect for a summer cocktail hour. There are many more just as easy and interesting—I'm sure you'll find your favorite.

Crabmeat Canapés

Nantucket House of Chatham Bed & Breakfast
South Chatham, Massachusetts
www.chathaminn.com

A canapé is a small cracker or small slice of bread
or toast cut into various fun shapes and garnished
with a creative flair—anything from cheese, to
herbs, to edible flowers. It's festive and fun!

MAKES 32 CANAPÉS

4 ounces fresh lump crabmeat, picked over

2 tablespoons mayonnaise

1 tablespoon fresh lemon juice

2 tablespoons finely chopped celery

2 tablespoons finely chopped green bell pepper

2 large hard-boiled eggs, finely chopped

$^{1}/_{2}$ teaspoon Tabasco

$^{1}/_{4}$ teaspoon paprika

8 slices homemade-type white bread

2 tablespoons fine fresh bread crumbs

$^{1}/_{4}$ cup ($^{1}/_{2}$ stick) butter, melted

1. In a medium bowl, stir together the crabmeat, mayonnaise, lemon juice, celery, bell pepper, hard-boiled eggs, Tabasco, and paprika. Cover and refrigerate overnight.

The next day

2. Toast the bread, and cut off and discard the crusts. Cut each slice into 4 triangles.

3. Preheat the broiler. Spread the crab mixture on the toasts and sprinkle with the bread crumbs. Drizzle with the melted butter. Broil the canapés on a baking sheet about 4 inches from the heat until they are golden brown.

Shrimp Rémoulade

Nantucket House of Chatham Bed & Breakfast
South Chatham, Massachusetts
www.chathaminn.com

Low in calories, shrimp is always a hit. To cook fresh shrimp, drop into boiling stock or water. Reduce the heat at once and simmer for 3 to 4 minutes. Drain immediately. This makes a huge amount of shrimp, but it is delicious.

SERVES 20

4 cups vegetable oil

1 jar (12 ounces) horseradish-flavored mustard

$^1/_4$ cup white wine vinegar

1 tablespoon sugar

2 tablespoons prepared horseradish

Tabasco

Salt and freshly ground black pepper

$^1/_2$ cup finely chopped parsley

2 cups finely chopped celery

1 cup finely chopped scallions

10 pounds medium shrimp, shelled

Lemon wedges, for garnish

1. Half fill a large pot with water and place over high heat to bring to a boil. In a large bowl, combine the oil, mustard, vinegar, sugar, horseradish, and Tabasco to taste. Season to taste with salt and pepper. Add the parsley, celery, and scallions and mix well.

2. Add the shrimp to the boiling water and cook just until opaque; be careful not to overcook. Drain immediately and transfer to the bowl of oil and seasonings; mix well. Cover and refrigerate overnight.

The next day

3. Serve over ice. Garnish with lemon wedges and serve with fancy toothpicks.

Hot Crab Dip

Belle Reve Bed & Breakfast
Riverton, Pennsylvania
www.bellereveriverside.com

As a former "Joisey Girl" relocated to the Pocono Mountains of Pennsylvania, I arrived with plenty of recipes for seafood dishes from the beautiful Jersey Shore. This is one of my favorites as well as a favorite of our guests. It is easy, and the taste brings me back to the shore—minus the sand and seagulls, of course!—SHIRLEY CREO, INNKEEPER

SERVES 8 TO 10

8 ounces cream cheese
2 teaspoons milk
2 teaspoons grated onion
1 teaspoon prepared horseradish
4 ounces fresh crabmeat
Slivered almonds, to taste
Sturdy crackers, for serving

1. In a small mixing bowl, combine the cream cheese, milk, onion, and horseradish; mix well. Add the crabmeat and fold together until thoroughly blended. Transfer to a 3-cup ovenproof glass baking dish. Cover and refrigerate overnight.

The next day

2. Preheat the oven to 350°F. Sprinkle the dip with the almonds and bake until well heated, about 20 minutes. Serve hot with crackers.

Spicy Sausage Meatballs

Nantucket House of Chatham Bed & Breakfast
South Chatham, Massachusetts
www.chathaminn.com

Our friend Stephanie was inn-sitting for us while we attended our son's wedding. We had a house full of guests and Stephanie thought it would be nice to do a cocktail hour over the weekend. She spoiled everyone by serving these meatballs. Upon our return, our guests continued to compliment Steph, her meatballs, and the now much-acclaimed cocktail hour!—C.G.

MAKES ABOUT 24 MEATBALLS

$^1/_2$ pound sharp Cheddar cheese, grated

1 pound spicy sausage, crumbled

2 cups Bisquick

$^1/_2$ teaspoon celery seed

Hot sauce

Garlic powder

Salt and freshly ground black pepper

1. In a large bowl, mix together the cheese, sausage, Bisquick, and celery seed. Season to taste with hot sauce, garlic powder, and salt and pepper. Cover and refrigerate overnight.

The next day

2. Preheat the oven to 375°F. Roll the mixture into 1-inch balls and place on a baking sheet. Bake until browned, about 15 to 20 minutes.

Maggi's Famous Blue Cheese Ball

Nantucket House of Chatham Bed & Breakfast
South Chatham, Massachusetts
www.chathaminn.com

My friend Stephanie opened her recipe files to me.
I feel as if Stephanie is as much an innkeeper of
the Nantucket House as we are. She's always
thinking of cute items for the inn, and has recently
discovered her talent for creating novelty items
that fit our decor so well: cute shelves, trivets,
napkin rings, and so on. Maggi, Stephanie's mom,
was the creator of this best cheese ball ever!—C.G.

SERVES 6 TO 8

2 packages (8 ounces each) regular or low-fat cream cheese,
at room temperature

1 cup your favorite blue cheese, crumbled

$1/4$ cup grated onion

1 tablespoon prepared horseradish

Salt and freshly ground black pepper to taste

$1^1/2$ cups chopped walnuts or pecans, as needed

1. In the bowl of an electric mixer, combine the cream
cheese, blue cheese, onion, and horseradish. Season with
salt and pepper to taste and mix until smooth. Cover and
refrigerate overnight.

The next day

2. For the best flavor and texture, coat the cheese ball with nuts no more than 3 hours before serving. To coat with nuts, spread the nuts across a sheet of wax paper or foil. Mound the cheese mixture in the center and shape into a ball, patting the nuts all over it. Transfer to a serving plate. Cover and refrigerate until a half hour before serving.

Artichoke Spinach Dip

Nantucket House of Chatham Bed & Breakfast
Chatham, Massachusetts
www.chathaminn.com

My friend's mother lived in the artichoke center of
the world—Castroville, California. This is how she
taught me to prepare artichokes : Choose nice firm
artichokes that are not turning brown. You'll need
two large bowls—one containing cold water and
the juice of 2 lemons ; the other, just cold water.
Keep the artichokes in the bowl of only cold water.
Take one artichoke out of the bowl of cold water,
drain it, and pull off and discard the small outer
leaves. Holding the artichoke with its bottom toward the little finger of your hand, tilt the top away
from you and hold a small knife tightly with your
right hand. Insert the knife into the top of one leaf
deep into the tender, lighter part of the leaves.
Keeping your right hand steady, rotate the
artichoke with your left hand so the bottom moves
in a clockwise direction. Cut upward in a spiral pattern. The tough part of each leaf will fall off, while
the tender edible part remains attached. Peel the
green layer off the bottom and stem, and then
place the artichoke into the lemon water until
ready to cook. This takes practice—the peeled
artichoke should more or less look like the one you
started with, only smaller and whiter. Or you can
just purchase a jar of artichokes in your local
supermarket! Remember, the fuzzy thing in the
center called a *choke* is not edible.—C.G.

8 ounces light cream cheese (do not use fat-free), at room
temperature

$^1/_4$ cup mayonnaise

$^1/_4$ cup grated or shredded Parmesan cheese

$^1/_4$ cup grated or shredded Romano cheese

2 teaspoons minced onion (optional)

1 garlic clove, peeled and minced

$^1/_2$ teaspoon dried basil or 1 tablespoon chopped fresh basil

$^1/_4$ teaspoon garlic salt

1 can (14 ounces) artichoke hearts, drained and chopped

$^1/_2$ cup frozen spinach, thawed, drained, and chopped

Nonstick vegetable oil spray

$^1/_4$ cup grated or shredded mozzarella cheese

1. In a large mixing bowl, cream together the cream
cheese, mayonnaise, Parmesan and Romano cheeses, onion
(if using), minced garlic, basil, and garlic salt. Add the artichokes and spinach; mix until well blended. Store the mixture in a tightly sealed bowl and refrigerate overnight.

The next day

2. Preheat the oven to 350°F. Spray a 9-inch glass pie pan
with the cooking spray. Spread the dip in pan and top with
the mozzarella. Bake until well heated, about 25 minutes.

Chicken Liver Pâté

Thistle and Shamrock Inn
Bradford, New Hampshire
(Thistle and Shamrock is no longer operating as an inn.)

How many times have you tried to make *the* perfect chicken liver pâté? Stress no more—this recipe is wonderful and loved by all! Serve it with water crackers, flatbreads, or bagel chips.

SERVES 8 TO 10

12 ounces bacon, diced

2 large onions, peeled and diced

4 garlic cloves, peeled and chopped

4 bay leaves

4 whole cloves

1 scant teaspoon dried thyme leaves

$1/2$ teaspoon dried oregano leaves

$1^3/4$ pounds fresh chicken livers

7 large eggs, beaten

$3/4$ cup ($1^1/2$ sticks) butter, softened

1 teaspoon Maggi seasoning

4 teaspoons Worcestershire sauce

$1/2$ teaspoon Tabasco

Salt and freshly ground black pepper

1. Preheat the oven to 500°F. In a flameproof casserole dish over medium-low heat, sauté the bacon until it begins to release fat. Add the onions, garlic, bay leaves, cloves, thyme, and oregano. Sauté until the onions are soft and the bacon is thoroughly cooked but still soft. Add the chicken livers and continue to sauté until the livers are browned on the outside and slightly pink in the centers.

2. Bake the casserole, uncovered, for 10 minutes, stirring occasionally. Stir the eggs into the chicken liver mixture and leave in the oven 10 more minutes. Remove from the oven and discard the bay leaves and cloves. Cool, transfer to a food processor, and process until smooth. Cover and refrigerate overnight.

The next day

3. Place the liver mixture in a mixing bowl fitted with a whisk attachment. Whisk on medium speed for 10 minutes. Add the softened butter and whisk an additional 10 minutes. Season with the Maggi, Worcestershire sauce, Tabasco, and salt and pepper to taste. Chill thoroughly before serving.

Smoked Salmon or Brie Herb Cheese Egg Puff

Otters Pond Bed & Breakfast
Orcas Island, Washington
www.otterspond.com

The Pacific Northwest is noted for salmon. As innkeepers, we love to use foods native to our area. We came up with this recipe using our local salmon and added the Brie herb cheese for wonderful flavor. Be careful, the egg puff is very hot! You can substitute a pasteurized egg equivalent for the eggs.

—CARL & SUSAN SILVERNAIL, INNKEEPERS

SERVES 6

10 large eggs

$1/2$ cup milk

$1/2$ cup 2% fat cottage cheese

6 ounces cream cheese

$1/2$ teaspoon salt

$1/4$ teaspoon freshly ground black pepper

Dried dill

2 tablespoons dried onion flakes

$1/2$ teaspoon fines herbes (or a pinch of thyme, oregano, rosemary, basil, and sage mix)

Nonstick vegetable oil spray

6 tablespoons flaked smoked salmon or about $2/3$ cup creamed herbed Brie cheese

1. In a large bowl, combine the eggs, milk, cottage cheese, and cream cheese. Add the salt, pepper, dill to taste, onion flakes, and fines herbes. Use a potato masher to incorporate the cream cheese, leaving the mixture a little lumpy. Cover and refrigerate overnight.

The next day

2. Preheat the oven to 350°F. Spray six individual 1-cup ramekins with vegetable oil spray and fill each with ³/₄ cup of the egg mixture. Mix in 1 tablespoon smoked salmon and/or drop in 4 or 5 teaspoons creamed Brie. Bake for 18 to 20 minutes, until puffed and just firm in the center when gently shaken. Test by inserting a knife between the egg puff and the dish; when pressing gently toward the center, the egg should not leak out. These puff up like a soufflé; serve immediately.

Nantucket House
Six-Layer Dip

Nantucket House of Chatham Bed & Breakfast
South Chatham, Massachusetts
www.chathaminn.com

We had a wedding party staying with us. Everything was going smoothly until the maid of honor arrived with a small dog in a carrier. Normally, we don't take dogs in the inn. Unfortunately, their pet care arrangements had fallen through and they had no place to leave their pet. They requested that their dog be allowed to remain in their room at night. Our inn was full, but we took a deep breath and said yes. The dog totally captivated us, and we had a great time playing and walking him with our dog. Our policy now is: "If your dog will vouch for you, you're welcome at the Nantucket House."—C.G.

This dip is perfect for many cocktail or informal parties. You may want to try a seventh layer using refried beans on the bottom, then avocados.

SERVES 8 TO 10

2 packages (1.25 ounces each) taco seasoning mix

4 tablespoons mayonnaise

6 tablespoons sour cream

4 avocados

2 bunches scallions, trimmed and chopped

3 tomatoes, cored and diced

2 cans (3.8 ounces each) sliced black olives

2 cups shredded Cheddar cheese
Tortilla chips, for serving

1. In a small bowl, combine the taco seasoning, 1 tablespoon mayonnaise, and the sour cream; mix well. Cover and refrigerate overnight.

The next day

2. Mash the avocados with the remaining 3 tablespoons mayonnaise and spread on the bottom of a 4-cup bowl. Top with the refrigerated taco mix, then the chopped scallions. Spread the diced tomatoes over the scallions and top with the sliced black olives. Sprinkle the shredded Cheddar cheese over all. Refrigerate until ready to serve. Serve with the chips.

Super Bowl Meatballs

Nantucket House of Chatham Bed & Breakfast
South Chatham, Massachusetts
www.chathaminn.com

I've taken these to so many Super Bowl parties. So easy and so good, they're always a hit! The grape jelly is not a typo—it really works in the sauce. You'll see. . . . —COURTNEY BLANKENSHIP

SERVES 6

One jar (12 ounces) Concord grape jelly

1 cup ketchup

2 tablespoons yellow mustard

2 tablespoons Worcestershire sauce

One package (2 pounds) cocktail-size frozen meatballs

1. In a Crock-Pot, combine the jelly, ketchup, mustard, and Worcestershire sauce. Add the meatballs and mix again. Cover the Crock-Pot and turn on High. Allow the mixture to heat until the meatballs are bubbling and the sauce is smooth, about 1 hour. Reduce the heat to Low for 10 to 15 minutes.

2. Allow the mixture to cool. Cover and refrigerate overnight.

The next day

3. Return the meatballs to the Crock-Pot and cook on High until reheated. Reduce the heat to its lowest setting and serve the meatballs warm from the Crock-Pot.

Chili Cheese Puff

Nantucket House of Chatham Bed & Breakfast
South Chatham, Massachusetts
www.chathaminn.com

Depending on how much you like chilies, you can
use either a 4- or 7-ounce can in this recipe. To
achieve a nice creamed cottage cheese, purée
the cottage cheese in a blender.

SERVES 4 TO 6

Butter, for greasing the pie plate
1 cup small-curd cottage cheese
5 large eggs
$1/2$ teaspoon baking powder
$1/4$ cup all-purpose flour
$1/4$ teaspoon salt
8 ounces shredded Monterey Jack cheese or a mixture of
Cheddar and Monterey Jack cheeses
4 tablespoons ($1/2$ stick) butter, melted
1 can (4 or 7 ounces) diced green chilies, drained

1. Thickly butter a 9-inch glass pie plate or other shallow
baking dish; set aside. Place the cottage cheese in a blender
and blend at low speed until smooth; set aside.

2. In a mixing bowl, beat the eggs until light and lemon-
colored. Add the baking powder, flour, salt, cheese, melted
butter, and blended cottage cheese; mix well.

3. Preheat the oven to 350°F. Stir the chilies into the egg
mixture and pour into the glass pie plate. Bake until set

and lightly browned, about 30 minutes. Cool. Cover and refrigerate overnight.

The next day

4. Remove the pie plate from the refrigerator and set aside at room temperature for about 20 minutes. Preheat the oven to 350°F. Bake until slightly puffed and golden brown on top, 15 to 20 minutes. Serve warm.

Jellied Shrimp

Commodore Joshua Barney House
Historic Savage, Maryland
www.joshuabarneyhouse.com

This is an old family recipe that is delicious as either a luncheon main course or an appetizer spread on crackers.—SUSAN BETTS, INNKEEPER

SERVES 10 TO 12

1 envelope plain gelatin

1 can condensed tomato soup

8 ounces cream cheese, at room temperature

2 to 3 pounds medium or large peeled and cooked shrimp

1 1/2 cups finely diced celery

1/2 cup finely chopped onion

1/4 cup finely chopped green bell pepper

1 cup mayonnaise, plus additional for greasing the bowl

Iceberg lettuce leaves (optional)

Crackers, for serving

1. In a small dish, soak the gelatin in ¹/₂ cup of cold water. In a large saucepan, heat to boiling the undiluted tomato soup. Add the cream cheese to the soup and whisk together until blended. Set the mixture aside, allowing it to cool slightly (do not refrigerate).

2. If serving as a main course, leave the shrimp whole; if serving as an appetizer, chop the shrimp coarsely. In a large bowl, mix the celery, onion, green pepper, and shrimp. Add 1 cup mayonnaise and mix.

3. Add the gelatin mixture to the soup mixture and then add the shrimp mixture; stir well. Pour into a large bowl or mold greased with mayonnaise. Cover and refrigerate overnight.

The next day

4. To serve as a main course, arrange iceberg lettuce leaves on plates and top with a mound of jellied shrimp; serve with crackers. To serve as an appetizer, spread on crackers.

Kelly's Cheese Spread

Nantucket House of Chatham Bed & Breakfast
South Chatham, Massachusetts
www.chathaminn.com

Kelly and Bobby were guests of the Nantucket House of Chatham. When they heard I was doing a cookbook, Kelly promptly sent me several recipes to share. We've had fun surprising our guests with many of her recipes. I know you'll use this cheese spread recipe over and over again.—C.G.

(All of the cheeses used here can be found in the dairy department of the supermarket.)

SERVES 8 TO 10

8 ounces cream cheese, at room temperature

Two containers WisPride Cheddar cheese,
at room temperature

1 jar (5 ounces) Kraft Roka Blue cheese,
at room temperature

1 garlic clove, peeled and minced

$1/4$ cup minced onion

About 1 cup chopped walnuts, or as needed

1. Using an electric mixer, blend together the cream cheese, WisPride Cheddar, Roka Blue cheese, garlic, and onion in a large bowl. Transfer to a covered container and refrigerate overnight.

The next day

2. Spread the walnuts across a sheet of wax paper or plastic wrap. Mound the cheese mixture in the center of the nuts and pat it into a ball. Roll the cheese ball in the chopped walnuts, lifting the edges of the paper to bring the nuts over the sides of the ball and then help roll it over.

3. Transfer the nut-covered ball to a plate. Cover and refrigerate until serving.

Sausage Puff

A Yellow Rose Bed & Breakfast
San Antonio, Texas
www.ayellowrose.com

This is also delicious with other stuffings—
scrambled eggs, a mixture of chopped artichoke
hearts and cream cheese, or a mixture of
scrambled eggs and bacon—or create your own.

SERVES 4

Vegetable oil or nonstick vegetable oil spray
1 can (8 ounces) refrigerated crescent rolls
8 ounces bulk sausage
5 tablespoons cream cheese
1 large egg white
2 tablespoons sesame seeds

1. Oil or spray a baking sheet. Spread half the crescent roll dough on a greased cookie sheet, pinching the seams to make one piece of dough.

2. In a large nonstick skillet, fry the sausage until cooked and crumbled. Add the cream cheese to the pan while the meat is still warm and stir until completely mixed.

3. Spread the sausage mixture over the crescent dough to within an inch of the edges. Cover with the other half of the crescent dough and crimp the edges neatly. Cover with plastic wrap and refrigerate overnight.

The next day

4. Preheat the oven to 350°F. Rub the egg white over the top of the dough and sprinkle with the sesame seeds. Bake until firm and golden brown, 10 to 15 minutes.

Tchoupitoulas
(Chop-a-TOO-lus)
Chicken Wings

Avenue Inn Bed & Breakfast
New Orleans, Louisiana
www.avenueinnbb.com

Mardi Gras, friends, family, inn guests, and twenty-four-hour partying! This recipe was born out of necessity to provide a last-minute grill item during Mardi Gras several years ago. Chicken wings came from an all-night grocery on Tchoupi-toulas Street. That night a guest asked me the name of these wings and I quickly said Tchoupitoulas Wings. The recipe is easily multiplied. You'll be amazed at how much flavor these wings have! Tchoupitoulas Wings have now become a tradition in their own right!
—JOE & BEBE RABHAN, INNKEEPERS

SERVES 6

2 pounds fresh or frozen chicken wings

3 teaspoons Tabasco

1 teaspoon Chef Paul Prudhomme's Magic Meat
seasoning blend

Vegetable oil or nonstick vegetable oil spray,
for oven baking

1. Place the wings in a bowl or a plastic storage bag. Add the Tabasco and meat seasoning and stir to coat well. Cover or seal and refrigerate overnight.

The next day

2. To grill: Preheat a grill on low to medium heat. Grill, turning once, until the juice from inside the thicker pieces runs clear, 10 to 15 minutes per side.

To bake: Preheat the oven to 400°F. Cover a sheet pan with foil and coat with vegetable oil. Place the wings on the pan in a single layer. Bake, turning once, until the juice from the thicker pieces runs clear, 10 to 15 minutes per side.

The First Lady's Cheese Spread

The Governor's Inn
Ludlow, Vermont
www.thegovernorsinn.com

After you've skied all day on Okemo Mountain, Vermont, you're ready for this popular appetizer. One of our most requested appetizers, it's called

The First Lady's Cheese Spread in honor of the
wife of Governor Stickney, who built the inn
in 1890.—CATHY KUBEC, INNKEEPER

SERVES 2

1/2 cup dry white wine
Juice of 2 lemons
1/4 cup freshly snipped chives
1 tablespoon freshly ground white pepper
3 garlic cloves, peeled and minced
2 tablespoons dried basil
2 teaspoons marjoram
4 packages (8 ounces each) cream cheese
Crackers, for serving

1. In a small saucepan, combine the wine, lemon juice, chives, white pepper, garlic, basil, and marjoram. Simmer over low heat for 15 minutes.

2. Place the wine mixture in a food processor with the cream cheese and process until blended. Transfer to a bowl, cover, and refrigerate overnight.

The next day
3. Serve at room temperature with crackers.

Mushroom Rolls

Nantucket House of Chatham Bed & Breakfast
South Chatham, Massachusetts
www.chathaminn.com

I make these and keep them in the freezer to have
on hand. You can also put a very small amount of
finely chopped onion in with the mushrooms or add
chives with the lemon juice. I took these to my
friend's bridal shower, and they were devoured in
a minute. Another variation is to put the mixture
into frozen phyllo shells and serve as mini-tarts
—very cute!—COURTNEY BLANKENSHIP

SERVES 12

1 loaf sliced white bread, crusts removed
$^1\!/_2$ cup (1 stick) butter
8 ounces fresh mushrooms, finely chopped
Salt
3 tablespoons flour
1 cup light cream
1 tablespoon lemon juice

1. Using a rolling pin, gently roll out the bread slices to
about $^1\!/_8$-inch thickness.

2. Place a large skillet over medium-low heat and melt 4
tablespoons of the butter. Add the mushrooms and sauté
until soft. Season to taste with salt and sprinkle in the
flour, stirring to blend. Add the cream and stir for 1
minute, until the mixture is slightly thickened. Stir in the
lemon juice.

3. Spread equal portions of the mushroom mixture on the bread slices and roll up like a jelly roll. Wrap airtight and refrigerate overnight.

The next day

4. Preheat the oven to 400°F. In a saucepan or in the microwave, melt the remaining 4 tablespoons butter. Place the rolls, seam-side down, on a baking sheet and brush with the melted butter. Bake until golden, 5 to 10 minutes.

Breakfast

Take it from someone who has served well over 1,800 breakfasts at the Nantucket House of Chatham. I am always looking for new exciting recipes. I find if it's fun for me to prepare, the guests enjoy it even more. The Baked Blueberry French Toast on page 35 is one of our favorites here at the Nantucket House.

Six-Week Raisin Bran Muffins

House on the Hill Bed & Breakfast
Harwich, Massachusetts
(House on the Hill is no longer operating as a bed-and-breakfast.)

Before our first season of innkeeping, I decided to introduce myself to the neighboring inns. Our neighbors were gracious, showed me their inns, and wished us well. One innkeeper invited me in and told me she would give me one of the best gifts an innkeeper could receive—this recipe. She was right! This muffin mix can be refrigerated up to six weeks in a nonmetallic container. These flavorful muffins are moist and always a treat, especially with our health-conscious guests. This recipe has helped me on the frequent occasions when guests appear during our downtime, and when neighborhood functions request a baked item.
—C.G.

MAKES ENOUGH FOR 48 MUFFINS

5 cups all-purpose flour

3 cups sugar, plus additional for sprinkling

5 teaspoons baking soda

$1^1/_2$ teaspoons salt

$7^1/_2$ cups (20-ounce box) Post Healthy Classics Raisin Bran

4 cups (1 quart) buttermilk

1 cup vegetable oil

4 large eggs, beaten

Vegetable cooking oil spray
Melted butter, for brushing the tops of the muffin batter
Ground cinnamon and sugar mixed

1. In a very large bowl or pot, combine the flour, 3 cups sugar, the baking soda, and salt. Stir in the cereal, add the buttermilk, oil, and eggs, and blend until moistened. Do not stir again. Place the mixture into a nonmetallic container, seal tightly, and refrigerate overnight or for up to 6 weeks.

When ready to bake

2. Preheat the oven to 400°F. Spray a 12-cup muffin pan with cooking oil spray. Fill each cup three-quarters full with batter. Brush the top of the batter in each cup with melted butter and sprinkle with cinnamon and sugar to taste. Bake until risen and firm, 15 to 20 minutes.

Baked Blueberry French Toast

The Village Inn at Sandwich Center
Sandwich, Massachusetts
www.belfryinn.com

This story tells you just how easy this recipe is to make. Friends of ours with a new baby came for a visit. I had made this blueberry French toast and had it in the refrigerator for the next morning. Late that night, Michael came down to get the baby's bottle out of the fridge. The fridge was full; when he reached for the bottle (at 3:00 A.M.), the blueberry French toast crashed to the floor, breaking the covered baking dish. He was devastated. He noticed that I had the recipe on the counter, so after feeding the baby, he came back into the kitchen and prepared a new dish of the French toast. What a great guy! Breakfast went off without a hitch, thanks to Michael. This is now one of their favorite recipes as well. —C.G.

SERVES 6

1 loaf Italian bread

4 large eggs

$^1/_2$ cup milk

$^1/_4$ teaspoon baking powder

1 teaspoon pure vanilla extract

Nonstick vegetable oil spray

$2^1/_2$ cups blueberries

$^1/_2$ cup cranberries (optional)

$^1/_2$ cup sugar

1 teaspoon ground cinnamon

1 teaspoon cornstarch

2 tablespoons butter, melted

$^1/_4$ cup confectioners' sugar

1. Slice the bread on the diagonal to create eight $^3/_4$-inch-thick slices, heels removed and discarded. Place the bread slices in a single layer or slightly overlapping in a 10 × 15-inch glass baking dish.

2. In a medium bowl, combine the eggs, milk, baking powder, and vanilla and whisk until smooth. Slowly pour the mixture over the bread, turning over each slice to coat completely. Cover and refrigerate overnight.

The next day

3. Preheat the oven to 425°F. Coat another 10 × 15-inch glass baking dish with nonstick spray, or transfer the bread to a platter and wash and spray the dish they were in. Sprinkle the blueberries and cranberries (if using) over the bottom of the pan. Mix together the sugar, cinnamon, and cornstarch in a small bowl and pour evenly over the berries.

4. Tightly wedge the bread slices over the blueberries, wettest side up. Brush the bread with the melted butter. Bake the French toast in the center of the oven until golden brown, 20 to 25 minutes.

5. To serve, place the toast, berry-side down, on warmed plates. Stir the berry mixture remaining in the baking dish, then scoop over the toast. Sprinkle with the confectioners' sugar before serving.

Southwest Strata

Garth Woodside Mansion Bed & Breakfast
Hannibal, Missouri
www.garthmansion.com

You can easily add other veggies, such as fresh
corn, to this strata. Omit the meat and add a few
more mushrooms for vegetarian guests.
Sometimes I'll surprise the guests by chopping
tofu and adding it to the strata. They don't realize
they're eating something healthy until I tell them.
You should see the looks on their faces!
—JULIE ROLSEN, INNKEEPER

SERVES 10 TO 12

Nonstick vegetable oil spray

3 flour tortillas (12 inches each)

1 cup refried beans

6 mushrooms, sliced

1 pound ground chorizo or Italian or turkey sausage,
cooked and crumbled

2 scallions, chopped

2 cups chopped dry fresh spinach

6 large eggs

$1/2$ cup whole milk

1 cup shredded Cheddar cheese

1 cup shredded mozzarella cheese

Chopped cilantro, for garnish

1 cup sour cream

$1/2$ cup mild salsa

1. Thoroughly coat the bottom of a 9 × 13-inch glass baking dish with the nonstick spray. Cut one tortilla in half. Place the 2 whole tortillas on either end and each of the halves of the third tortilla in the middle, putting the curved side in the middle of the dish, to cover the bottom of the dish.

2. Spoon the beans on the tortillas and top with the mushrooms, sausage, scallions, and spinach. Beat the eggs with the milk in a large mixing bowl and pour over all. Sprinkle the Cheddar and mozzarella cheeses over the entire pan. Cover and refrigerate overnight.

The next day

3. Preheat the oven to 350°F. Bake the strata, uncovered, until lightly browned, about 45 minutes. (If the strata is browning too quickly, cover it with foil.)

4. To serve, sprinkle the strata with cilantro. In a small bowl, mix together the sour cream and salsa to pass separately at the table.

Twin Oaks Sticky Buns

Twin Oaks Inn
Saugatuck, Michigan
www.bbonline.com/mi/twinoaks

Every once in a while, a woman I worked with would bring these delicious sticky buns into work as a treat. When I became a bed-and-breakfast owner, I knew this was a recipe I had to have. One of the best things about this recipe is that, if you keep the ingredients on hand, it's easy to accommodate those surprise guests.

—WILLA LAMKEN, INNKEEPER

SERVES 18

Vegetable oil or nonstick vegetable oil spray

$^1/_2$ to $^3/_4$ cup pecans, as desired

18 frozen unbaked white dinner rolls (available in bags in the supermarket freezer)

1 box (3.8 ounces) butterscotch cook-and-serve pudding and pie filling

$^1/_4$ cup brown sugar

$^1/_2$ cup (1 stick) butter, melted

1. Oil or spray a bundt pan. Sprinkle the pecans in the bottom of the pan. Arrange the frozen rolls on top of the pecans.

2. Sprinkle the butterscotch pudding and brown sugar over the rolls. Pour the melted butter over all. Cover and place in a cold oven overnight or up to 12 hours.

The next day

3. Remove the rolls before preheating the oven to 350°F. Bake the rolls, uncovered, until risen and golden brown, 15 to 20 minutes. Invert onto a plate immediately after removing from the oven. Let cool slightly; serve warm.

Bananas Foster French Toast

The Duke of Windsor Inn
Cape May, New Jersey
www.dukeofwindsorinn.com

We were early into our innkeeping experience when a couple was ready to check out. We were all talking on the deck and they offered us their credit card. Oops, the card went down into the crack in the deck. My husband literally had to crawl under the deck—not an easy feat—and retrieve the credit card. We all had a lot of laughs—no extra charge!—C.G.

SERVES 12

FOR THE FRENCH TOAST
Nonstick vegetable oil spray

$1^1/_2$ loaves narrow French bread, thinly sliced

6 large eggs

$^3/_4$ cup granulated sugar

2 cups half-and-half

2 cups milk

4 teaspoons pure vanilla extract

1 teaspoon ground cinnamon

FOR THE FILLING
12 ounces cream cheese

$^1/_4$ cup granulated sugar

2 large eggs

$^1/_2$ cup brown sugar
4 tablespoons ($^1/_2$ stick) butter
2 tablespoons heavy cream
$^3/_4$ teaspoon rum extract
5 bananas, peeled and sliced

1. For the French toast, spray a 10 × 15-inch glass baking dish with the nonstick spray. Lay half the bread on the bottom to cover it entirely. In a large bowl, combine the eggs, sugar, half-and-half, milk, vanilla, and cinnamon. Whisk until well blended and reserve.

2. For the filling, combine the cream cheese, sugar, and eggs in a bowl, then spread over the bread in the baking dish. Arrange the remaining bread slices on top of the filling. Pour all the reserved liquid on top. (There will be a lot of liquid, but it all gets absorbed.) Cover and refrigerate overnight.

The next day

3. Preheat the oven to 350°F. Bake the French toast until it is puffy and light golden brown, 55 to 60 minutes. Remove from the oven and set aside to cool. Meanwhile, make the topping.

4. For the topping, combine the brown sugar, butter, heavy cream, and rum extract in a small saucepan. When the liquid is smooth and warm, add the bananas and continue cooking for 5 minutes. To serve, cut the French toast into squares and cover with the banana topping.

Guten Morgen Eggs

The Chalet Inn
Dillsboro, North Carolina
www.chaletinn.com

This dish will guarantee you a good morning in any
language! The recipe is very versatile; you can
change it according to the season: Vidalia onions in
the summer instead of scallions, dill weed instead
of parsley, cottage cheese instead of sour cream.
You may vary the cheeses as well.

SERVES 10

Vegetable oil or nonstick vegetable oil spray

16 large eggs

1 teaspoon grated nutmeg

Salt and freshly ground black pepper

1 tablespoon chopped fresh or dried parsley

$1/4$ cup finely chopped scallions

2 tablespoons ($1/4$ stick) butter

$1/2$ cup sour cream

8 to 12 mushrooms, sliced (optional)

2 cups grated sharp Cheddar cheese

1. Oil or spray two $9 \times 5 \times 3$-inch loaf pans or one 8-inch
square baking pan. In a large mixing bowl, beat the eggs
until frothy. Add the nutmeg, salt and pepper to taste,
parsley, and scallions.

2. Melt the butter in a large nonstick skillet over
medium heat. Pour in the egg mixture and scramble into
large wet curds. If using two baking dishes, divide the

scrambled eggs between the baking dishes and spread evenly in each. In the pan(s), add a layer of sour cream, mushrooms, and cheese. Cover and refrigerate overnight.

The next day

3. Preheat the oven to 325°F. Bake the eggs until the cheese has melted and is beginning to brown, about 30 minutes.

Bayou Bend Casserole

Nantucket House of Chatham Bed & Breakfast
South Chatham, Massachusetts
www.chathaminn.com

The Louisiana Bayou is not far from New Orleans.
Wake your guests up to a theme breakfast—
colorful linens, glass beads, a little zydeco music,
and this Cajun casserole!

SERVES 6 TO 8

Vegetable oil or nonstick vegetable oil spray
$^1/_2$ large loaf day-old French bread, torn into small pieces
3 tablespoons butter, melted
1 pound Monterey Jack cheese, shredded
$^1/_4$ pound Genoa salami, julienned
10 large eggs
$1^1/_2$ cups whole milk

$^{1}/_{3}$ cup white wine

3 large scallions, minced

2 teaspoons Dijon mustard

$^{1}/_{8}$ teaspoon coarsely ground black pepper

$^{1}/_{8}$ teaspoon red pepper flakes

1 cup sour cream

$^{1}/_{2}$ cup freshly grated Parmesan cheese

1. Oil or spray a 9 × 13-inch glass casserole dish. Spread the bread pieces over the bottom and drizzle with the melted butter. Sprinkle with the Monterey Jack cheese and salami pieces.

2. In a mixing bowl, put the eggs, milk, wine, scallions, mustard, black pepper, and red pepper flakes. Beat until the mixture is frothy. Pour the mixture over the bread pieces. Cover the casserole with foil and refrigerate overnight.

The next day

3. Remove from the refrigerator 30 minutes before baking. Preheat the oven to 325°F. Bake the casserole, covered, for 1 hour. Uncover, spread with the sour cream, and sprinkle with the Parmesan cheese. Bake, uncovered, until lightly browned, about 10 more minutes. Serve hot.

Blueberry-Stuffed French Toast

Vogt Farm Bed & Breakfast
Lancaster, Pennsylvania
www.vogtfarmbnb.com

This is another rendition of the classic favorite.
Enjoy! You can use fresh blueberries or jam. If
using jam, feel free to try other flavors. Rolling in
cornflakes is a little tricky, but it works. Try
serving as small individual French toasts
on a garnished platter.

SERVES 8 TO 10

1 loaf (1 pound) French bread, rounded ends removed

8 ounces cream cheese

1 pint blueberries

1½ cups milk

1½ cups half-and-half

7 large eggs

1½ teaspoons pure vanilla extract

½ cup sugar

Dash of grated nutmeg

¼ teaspoon ground cinnamon

Nonstick vegetable oil spray

2 cups crushed cornflakes

½ cup pecan pieces

Maple or other syrup, for serving

1. Slice the bread into $1/2$-inch-thick slices. Spread the cream cheese on one side of each slice. Lay half the bread slices in a 9×12-inch glass pan, cream cheese–side up. Put the blueberries on top of the cream cheese and top with the other slice of bread, cream cheese–side down.

2. In a large mixing bowl, combine the milk, half-and-half, eggs, vanilla, sugar, nutmeg, and cinnamon. Whisk together until well blended. Pour over the bread and let sit 5 minutes. Turn the slices over. Cover and refrigerate overnight.

The next day

3. Preheat oven to 350°F. Spray a baking sheet with non-stick spray and set aside. In a medium bowl, mix together the cornflakes and pecans. Roll each blueberry-stuffed piece in the cornflakes mixture and place on the baking sheet. Bake until light golden brown and crisp, about 30 minutes. Serve warm with maple syrup.

Crème Brûlée French Toast

Adirondack Pines Bed & Breakfast
Adirondack, New York
www.adirondackpines.com

A friend gave me this recipe when I first opened my bed-and-breakfast. This toast is quite decadent!—DAN & NANCY FREEBERN, INNKEEPERS

SERVES 6

$^1/_2$ cup (1 stick) unsalted butter

1 cup packed brown sugar

2 tablespoons corn syrup

1 round challah loaf (with or without raisins) or country-style bread, 8 to 9 inches in diameter

5 large eggs

1$^1/_2$ cups half-and-half

1 teaspoon pure vanilla extract

$^1/_2$ teaspoon salt

1 teaspoon Grand Marnier (optional)

Confectioners' sugar, for sprinkling

1. In a small, heavy saucepan, melt the butter with the brown sugar and corn syrup over moderate heat, stirring until smooth. Pour into a 13 × 9 × 2-inch glass baking dish..

2. Cut six 1-inch-thick slices from the center portion of the bread, reserving the ends for another use; trim off the crusts. Arrange the bread slices in one layer in the baking dish, squeezing them in slightly to fit. In a bowl, whisk together the eggs, half-and-half, vanilla, salt, and Grand Marnier (if using) until well combined. Pour evenly over the bread. Cover and refrigerate overnight.

The next day

3. Preheat the oven to 350°F and bring the bread to room temperature. Bake until firm and lightly golden on top, about 40 minutes. Sprinkle with confectioners' sugar, cut into squares, and serve.

Sunday Breakfast Casserole

Good Medicine Lodge
Whitefish, Montana
www.goodmedicinelodge.com

Native Americans in northwest Montana define
"good medicine" as "restoring balance with
oneself and nature." Betsy and Woody Cox, the
owners, have found that their guests restore
energy to them and their staff, as does their
proximity to Glacier National Park.

SERVES 10 TO 12

Butter, for greasing the baking dish

4 cups cubed day-old bread (bagels, English muffins, croissants)

1 cup mixed shredded cheese

9 large eggs

3 cups milk

1 teaspoon dry mustard

$1/2$ to 1 teaspoon garlic powder

$1/2$ cup crumbled blue cheese

$1/2$ cup cottage cheese

9 bacon strips, cooked and crumbled

4 ounces mushroom pieces

1 cup chopped onions

1. Butter a 9 × 13-inch glass baking dish. Spread the bread cubes across the bottom of the dish and sprinkle with the 1 cup mixed shredded cheese.

2. In a large bowl, combine the eggs, milk, dry mustard, and garlic powder. Add the blue cheese and cottage cheese and mix in. Pour the mixture over the bread and cheese. Sprinkle with the bacon, mushrooms, and onions. Cover and refrigerate overnight.

The next day

3. Preheat the oven to 350°F. Bake the casserole, uncovered, until golden brown on top, about 50 minutes. Serve warm.

Breakfast Egg Pizza

The Limestone Inn
Strasburg, Pennsylvania
www.thelimestoneinn.com

Our inn was first built for a local merchant in 1786. It housed the first Chief Burgess of Strasburg and the first post office in 1805. From 1839 to 1860, the principal of the Strasburg Academy boarded up to fifty boys attending the school that was erected behind the inn. I'm not sure if those boys were served this recipe, but if they were, I'm sure it would have been a favorite! If you prefer, you can make your own crust. This recipe is great for using up those ends of cheeses.

—KAREN PATZER, INNKEEPER

SERVES 6 TO 8

1 pound bulk sausage

$^1/_2$ cup thinly sliced onion

$^1/_2$ cup thinly sliced red or green bell pepper

1 package refrigerated crescent rolls

1 cup thinly sliced baked potatoes

1 cup shredded sharp Cheddar cheese

7 large eggs

Salt and freshly ground black pepper

Salsa, for serving

1. Place a large nonstick skillet over medium-high heat and brown the sausage. Transfer the sausage to a plate and drain most of the fat from the pan, saving some fat. Add the onion and pepper to the remaining fat and sauté until tender.

2. Roll out the crescent rolls so they lie flat in the bottom of a 10-inch pie plate, making sure the dough comes up the sides. Top with half the sausage, followed by half the peppers, half the onions, and half the potatoes. Top with half the cheese. Make another layer of sausage, peppers, onions, and potatoes, again topping with the cheese. Cover and refrigerate overnight.

The next day

3. Allow the pie plate to come to room temperature. Preheat the oven to 350°F. In a mixing bowl, beat the eggs until frothy and season to taste with salt and pepper. Pour the eggs into the pie plate. Bake until the eggs are set, about 30 minutes. Serve with salsa.

Buttermilk Oven Pancakes

The Duke of Windsor Inn
Cape May, New Jersey
www.dukeofwindsorinn.com

My husband always used to order pancakes when we would go out to breakfast. Try as I might, I could not make good pancakes—just ask my kids—so I would get a bite of his when we went out. All that has changed with this recipe! Not only do we not go out to breakfast as often, but now he says, "What will I order?"—C.G.

SERVES 8

FOR THE PANCAKES

Nonstick vegetable oil spray

2 cups flour

3 tablespoons sugar

1 teaspoon baking soda

1 teaspoon baking powder

$1/4$ teaspoon salt

1 large egg, beaten

$1 1/2$ cups buttermilk

3 tablespoons vegetable oil

FOR THE TOPPING

$1/2$ cup fresh blueberries or strawberries or 2 medium apples
or peaches, peeled, cored, and coarsely chopped

$1/4$ cup sugar

1 teaspoon ground cinnamon
Maple syrup, for serving

1. For the pancakes, spray a 9 × 13-inch baking pan with nonstick spray and set aside. In a mixing bowl, sift together the flour, sugar, baking soda, baking powder, and salt. In another bowl, mix together the egg, buttermilk, and oil; add to the dry ingredients and mix well.

2. Spread the batter evenly in the baking pan. Cover and refrigerate overnight.

The next day

3. Preheat the oven to 350°F.

4. For the topping, sprinkle the fruit over the top of the batter. In a small bowl, combine the sugar and cinnamon; sprinkle evenly over the fruit. Bake until the top springs back when lightly touched and is lightly browned around the edges, 25 to 30 minutes. Cut into square pancakes and serve with maple syrup.

Cinnamon Crunch Coffee Cake

The Inn at Schoolhouse Creek
Mendocino, California
www.schoolhousecreek.com

Inn Relief
Cresco, Pennsylvania
www.innrelief.com

This has to be *the* most famous overnight crunch coffee cake around! When soliciting recipes for this book, I actually received this recipe from two separate inns in California and Pennsylvania. And we have a similar recipe here at the Nantucket House. The topping may not appear to be enough, but it spreads out while baking and the melted brown sugar makes a nice crunch. If you can have comfort food for breakfast, this is it!—C.G.

SERVES 12 TO 16

FOR THE CAKE
Butter, for the baking dish
2 cups flour, plus additional for the baking dish
1 teaspoon baking powder
1 teaspoon baking soda
1 teaspoon ground cinnamon
1/4 teaspoon salt
2/3 cup butter or margarine, softened
1 cup granulated sugar
1/2 cup packed brown sugar
2 large eggs
1 cup buttermilk

FOR THE TOPPING

1/2 cup packed brown sugar
1/2 cup chopped walnuts
1/2 teaspoon ground cinnamon
1/4 teaspoon grated nutmeg

1. For the cake, butter and flour a 9 × 13-inch glass baking dish and set aside. Sift together 2 cups flour, the baking powder, baking soda, cinnamon, and salt. Using an electric mixer, cream together the butter and sugars in a large mixing bowl until light and fluffy. Add the eggs, one at a time, to the batter, beating well after each addition. Add the flour mixture alternately with the buttermilk to the butter mixture, beating well after each addition. Spread the batter in the baking dish.

2. For the topping, stir together the brown sugar, walnuts, cinnamon, and nutmeg in a small bowl. Sprinkle over the batter. Cover and refrigerate overnight.

The next day

3. Preheat the oven to 350°F and remove the cake from the refrigerator. Bake the cake, uncovered, until a toothpick inserted in the middle comes out clean, 35 to 40 minutes.

Croissants à L'Orange

Rosewood Country Inn
Bradford, New Hampshire
www.rosewoodcountryinn.com

If inns are ever really haunted, you could catch a
glimpse of Mary Pickford, Jack London, Douglas
Fairbanks, or the Gish sisters at the Rosewood
Country Inn. Perhaps they'll be dining on this
recipe! This is a very pretty dish—the marmalade
makes it glisten and the custard sets off the shape
of the croissant.—LESLEY MARQUIS, INNKEEPER

SERVES 6

Butter, for greasing the dishes

6 large croissants, cut into top and bottom halves

1 jar (18 ounces) orange marmalade

$1/3$ cup orange juice

5 large eggs

1 cup heavy cream

1 teaspoon pure almond extract

1 teaspoon finely grated orange zest

Orange slices, strawberries, and whipped cream,
for garnish

1. Butter six small ovenproof dishes just large enough to
hold a croissant. Place the bottom half of the croissant in
the dish.

2. In a bowl, combine the marmalade with the orange
juice and spoon 2 to 3 tablespoons over the croissant bot-
toms. Replace the tops.

3. In a mixing bowl, beat together the eggs, cream, almond extract, and orange zest. Pour about 3 tablespoons over each croissant top. Spoon 1 to 2 tablespoons of the remaining marmalade mixture over the top of each. Cover the dishes and refrigerate overnight.

The next day

4. Preheat the oven to 350°F. Bake the croissants, uncovered, until the liquid is set, 20 to 25 minutes. Allow to rest 5 minutes before serving. Garnish each with a slice of orange, a strawberry, and a tablespoon of whipped cream.

Ellie's Sunday Strata

Nantucket House of Chatham Bed & Breakfast
South Chatham, Massachusetts
www.chathaminn.com

IT'S NEVER TOO LATE TO BE A COWGIRL! My friend
Ellie sent me that bumper sticker when she moved
from Chatham to Colorado. The bumper sticker
remains as a constant reminder that it's never too
late for us to have fun and try new adventures.
I think of Ellie every day, especially when
I make this recipe.—C.G.

SERVES 12 TO 15

FOR THE CHEESE SAUCE

2 tablespoons (^{1}/$_4$ stick) butter or margarine
2^1/$_2$ tablespoons all-purpose flour
2 cups milk
^{1}/$_2$ teaspoon salt
^{1}/$_8$ teaspoon freshly ground black pepper
1 cup (4 ounces) shredded processed American cheese

FOR THE STRATA

Vegetable oil or nonstick vegetable oil spray
3 tablespoons butter or margarine
1 cup diced ham or Canadian bacon
^{1}/$_4$ cup chopped scallions
12 large eggs, beaten
^{1}/$_4$ pound sliced mushrooms
^{1}/$_4$ cup (^{1}/$_2$ stick) butter or margarine, melted
2^1/$_4$ cups soft bread crumbs
Paprika, as needed

1. For the cheese sauce, melt the butter in a heavy saucepan over low heat. Blend in the flour and cook 1 minute. Gradually add the milk; cook over medium heat until thickened, stirring constantly. Add the salt, pepper, and cheese, stirring until the cheese melts and the mixture is smooth. Remove from the heat and set aside.

2. Oil or spray a 9 × 13 × 2-inch glass baking dish and set aside. Melt 3 tablespoons butter in a large skillet and sauté the ham and scallions until the ham is lightly browned and the scallions are tender. Add the eggs and cook over medium-high heat, stirring to form large, soft curds. When the eggs are set, stir in the mushrooms and cheese sauce.

3. Spoon the egg mixture into the baking dish. Combine the melted butter and bread crumbs in a bowl, mixing well; spread evenly over the egg mixture. Sprinkle lightly with paprika. Cover and refrigerate overnight.

The next day

4. Preheat the oven to 350°F and remove the dish from the refrigerator. Uncover the dish and bake until heated thoroughly and lightly browned on top, about 30 minutes.

Walnut Carrot Raisin Muffins

Nantucket House of Chatham Bed and Breakfast
South Chatham, Massachusetts
www.chathaminn.com

Kelly and Bobby were guests at the Nantucket House. When they heard about our cookbook, they were very excited to participate and share favorite recipes. This recipe is very versatile and can be prepared as a bread or muffins.—C.G.

MAKES 12 MUFFINS

$^3/_4$ cup sugar

$5^1/_2$ tablespoons butter, melted

2 large eggs

2 cups all-purpose flour

3 teaspoons baking powder

$^1/_2$ teaspoon salt

$^1/_2$ teaspoon ground cinnamon

$1^1/_3$ cups grated carrots

$^3/_4$ cup chopped walnuts

$^1/_2$ cup raisins

Vegetable oil or nonstick vegetable oil spray

1. In a large bowl, cream together the sugar, butter, and eggs. Sift together the flour, baking powder, salt, and cinnamon. Add to the creamed mixture and stir until blended.

2. Add the carrots, walnuts, and raisins and fold together until blended. Cover and refrigerate overnight.

The next day

3. Preheat the oven to 400°F. Oil or spray a 12-cup muffin tin. Spoon the batter into the cups, filling two-thirds full. Bake until risen and dry in the center when tested with a toothpick, 20 to 25 minutes.

First Colony Juice Cordial

First Colony Inn
Nags Head, North Carolina
www.firstcolonyinn.com

This is a staple on our breakfast table every day—pretty, colorful, and refreshing! Not all the juices are readily available in local supermarkets, but a similar juice can be substituted for one that is not available. Try mixing this with champagne for a really nice punch.—CAMILLE LAWRENCE, MANAGER

SERVES 72

1 can (12 ounces) frozen white grape juice
1 can (12 ounces) frozen cranberry juice cocktail
1 can (12 ounces) frozen cranberry-raspberry juice cocktail
1 can (12 ounces) frozen cranberry-white grape juice
1 can (12 ounces) frozen raspberry-white grape juice
1 can (12 ounces) frozen passion fruit juice
Seltzer water, as needed, for serving

1. In a 2-gallon container, combine the juices with 2 cans of water each (a total of 4½ quarts of water if all six juices are used). Mix well and pour into several smaller jugs or containers. Refrigerate for up to 1 week.

Before serving

2. Mix 3 parts chilled juice to 1 part chilled seltzer water. Use 4-ounce cordial glasses placed on breakfast plates.

Nantucket House Upside-Down French Toast

Nantucket House of Chatham Bed & Breakfast
South Chatham, Massachusetts
www.chathaminn.com

My friend Julie got this recipe from her sister-in-law Shari, who got it from her mother. When we bought the inn, Julie gave it to me. One time, we had a father and his twelve-year-old daughter visiting with us from Texas. I served them Nantucket House Upside-Down French Toast for breakfast. They loved it and requested it again before they left with the recipe and a solemn promise from daughter to father to make the French toast for him frequently when they returned home to Texas.—C.G.

SERVES 6

1 cup packed brown sugar

$1/2$ cup (1 stick) butter

2 tablespoons white corn syrup

Challah or white bread, crusts removed

8 large eggs

2 teaspoons pure vanilla extract

$2^{1}/_{4}$ cups milk

Fresh fruit, for garnish

1. Combine the brown sugar, butter, and corn syrup in a large, heavy frying pan over medium heat. Stir until the butter melts and the sugar dissolves. Boil for 1 to 2 minutes, then pour into a 9 × 13-inch glass baking dish and tilt to coat the bottom of the pan.

2. Arrange the bread in two layers over the caramel. In a mixing bowl, combine the eggs, vanilla, and milk. Whisk to blend and pour over the bread. Cover with plastic wrap and refrigerate overnight.

The next day

3. Preheat the oven to 350°F. Bake the toast, uncovered, 40 to 60 minutes.

4. To serve, slice into portions and invert onto plates so that the syrupy side is on top. Garnish with fruit.

Oatmeal Brown Sugar Muffins

Sugar Hill Inn
Sugar Hill, New Hampshire
www.sugarhillinn.com

These muffins are so versatile. Any type of dry ingredient can be mixed into the batter—raisins, dried cranberries, chocolate chips. If fresh fruit is used, do not add it until you are ready to scoop and bake the muffins. Toss 1 cup of the fruit with 1 tablespoon flour, then fold into the mix.

MAKES 12 MUFFINS

1 cup all-purpose flour
1 cup packed brown sugar
1 cup rolled oats
1 teaspoon baking powder
$1/2$ teaspoon salt
1 cup sour cream
5 tablespoons butter, softened
2 large eggs
Nonstick vegetable oil spray

1. In a medium bowl, mix together the flour, brown sugar, oats, baking powder, and salt. In a separate bowl, combine the sour cream, butter, and eggs; mix well.

2. Add the wet ingredients to the dry ingredients and stir to blend. Cover and refrigerate overnight.

The next day

3. Preheat the oven to 375°F. Spray a 12-cup muffin pan with the nonstick spray. Bake until a toothpick inserted into the center of one muffin comes out clean, 20 to 30 minutes. Allow to cool for 10 minutes before removing from the pan.

Apple Oat Cakes

Asa Ransom House
Clarence, New York
www.asaransom.com

We like to feature as many local products as possible, and neighboring Niagara County is a big apple producer. So we put a little twist on pancakes and offer the Apple Oat Cakes with local maple syrup. Health-conscious guests also like the oats.

—BOB LENZ, INNKEEPER

MAKES 24 OAT CAKES

2 cups rolled oats

1 cup all-purpose flour

2 tablespoons sugar

2 teaspoons baking soda

1 tablespoon ground cinnamon

$1/2$ teaspoon ground ginger

$1/2$ teaspoon grated nutmeg

2 cups buttermilk

2 large eggs, beaten

1 apple, cored and minced

$1/4$ cup vegetable oil

Nonstick vegetable oil spray

1. In a large bowl, mix together the oats, flour, sugar, baking soda, cinnamon, ginger, and nutmeg.

2. Add the buttermilk, eggs, apple, and vegetable oil and mix well. Cover tightly and refrigerate overnight.

The next day

3. Spray a griddle with nonstick vegetable oil. Preheat the griddle or nonstick skillet to medium-high heat. Pour the batter by 1/4 cupfuls onto the hot griddle or skillet and allow to sit until set and lightly browned underneath, 1 to 2 minutes. Turn and cook until firm and lightly browned on the other side. Serve hot.

(Cooked oat cakes may be stored in an airtight container in the refrigerator and reheated in the oven or toaster.)

Praline French Bake

Inn at Lower Farm
North Stonington, Connecticut
www.lowerfarm.com

This French toast recipe has been used in our family for years. It's always the featured breakfast entrée at our large family gatherings. The glazed chopped pecans make a pretty topping.
—MARY WILSKA, INNKEEPER

SERVES 4

Butter, for greasing the pan
1 large loaf French bread, cut into 1-inch slices
6 large eggs
1 cup light cream
1½ cups milk
1 teaspoon pure vanilla extract

½ teaspoon ground cinnamon
½ teaspoon grated nutmeg
4 tablespoons butter, softened
½ cup dark brown sugar
½ cup chopped pecans
1 tablespoon light corn syrup
Maple syrup, for serving

1. Butter a 9-inch square glass baking pan. Arrange the bread slices close together in a single layer (so the slices touch) in the bottom of the pan. Using an electric mixer, combine the eggs, cream, milk, vanilla, cinnamon, and nutmeg in a mixing bowl. Pour the mixture over the bread. Cover and refrigerate overnight.

The next day

2. Preheat the oven to 350°F. In a small bowl, mix together the softened butter, brown sugar, pecans, and corn syrup and spread over the soaked bread. Bake until browned on top, about 30 minutes. Serve with warm maple syrup.

Schoolhouse Creek Breakfast Rolls

Inn at Schoolhouse Creek
Mendocino, California
www.schoolhousecreek.com

Making breakfast rolls from scratch always seemed so intimidating until I came to know the folks at the Inn at Schoolhouse Creek. I love this recipe and use it successfully to delight our guests at breakfast. They always think the rolls are much more difficult to make and I smile when they ask, "How do you do it?"—C.G.

SERVES 8 TO 10

FOR THE DOUGH

1/4 cup warm water (110 to 115°F)

1 teaspoon sugar

1 packet (1/4 ounce) active dry yeast

1 cup half-and-half

1 cup (2 sticks) butter, softened, plus additional for greasing the bowl

5 large egg yolks

3 cups sifted all-purpose flour

FOR THE FILLING

1/4 teaspoon salt

1/4 cup sugar

1 cup chopped almond slices

2 ounces almond paste, grated

1. For the dough, combine the warm water, sugar, and yeast in a small bowl. Set aside until foamy.

2. Place the half-and-half in a small saucepan over medium heat just until scalded (steaming, not bubbling). Let cool to lukewarm. Combine with the yeast mixture.

3. Using an electric mixer with a paddle attachment, in a mixing bowl, cream 1 cup butter until light and fluffy. Add the egg yolks, one at a time, and combine well after each addition. Alternately add the flour and yeast mixture to the creamed butter. Change to a dough hook and combine until the mixture comes away from the side of the mixer bowl. Grease a bowl with butter and add the dough, turning the dough to coat with the butter. Cover and chill overnight.

The next day

4. For the filling, mix the salt, sugar, chopped almonds, and almond paste in a small bowl. Place half the nut mixture on a lightly floured cutting board. Divide the dough in half and roll out to 1/8-inch thickness on top of the nut mixture, pressing in the nuts well. Place a sheet of parchment paper over the dough and turn over so the nuts are on top. Roll as for a jelly roll.

5. Line a baking sheet with parchment paper. Cut the rolled dough into 1/2-inch slices and place on the parchment-lined pan, leaving 1 inch of space between the rolls. Repeat the rolling process with the rest of the dough. Let rise until puffy, about 1 hour.

6. Preheat the oven to 350°F. Bake the rolls until lightly browned, about 20 minutes. Remove from the parchment and cool on a wire rack.

Southwestern Eggs

The Jefferson Inn
Jefferson, New Hampshire
www.jeffersoninn.com

**After eating this dish for breakfast, guests have
been known to pop the question while enjoying the
romantic views of the White Mountains.**

SERVES 6 TO 8

Nonstick vegetable oil spray

5 large eggs

$1/4$ cup all-purpose flour

$1/2$ teaspoon baking powder

Pinch of salt

2 cups (8 ounces) shredded Monterey Jack cheese

1 cup (8 ounces) nonfat cottage cheese

$1/4$ cup ($1/2$ stick) butter or margarine, melted

1 can (4 ounces) chopped green chilies, drained

1. Spray a 9-inch glass pie plate with the nonstick spray
and set aside. In a large bowl, beat the eggs until smooth.
Add the flour, baking powder, and salt and mix well. The
batter will appear lumpy.

2. Stir in the cheeses, melted butter, and green chilies
and mix thoroughly. Pour into the prepared pie plate.
Cover and refrigerate overnight.

The next day

3. Take the pie plate out of the refrigerator 20 minutes
prior to putting in the oven. Preheat the oven to 350°F.

Bake until the top just starts to turn golden brown, 35 to 40 minutes. Allow to set about 5 minutes before serving.

Toasted Pecan Corn Waffles

55 East Bed & Breakfast
Annapolis, Maryland
www.55east.com

These waffles are so tasty, they scarcely need any accompaniment. Since they aren't really sweet, they may also be used as a base for creamed mushrooms or chicken. I invented this recipe one day when I had lots of leftover cooked corn on the cob. Try garnishing the waffles with a dusting of confectioners' sugar and serve them warm with Canadian bacon and canned sliced peaches, drained and simmered with dark brown sugar.
—MAT & TRICIA HERBAN, INNKEEPERS

SERVES 8

6 large eggs, lightly beaten
2 cups whole milk, or more as needed
¾ cup (1½ sticks) butter, melted
2 tablespoons pure vanilla extract
4 cups all-purpose flour

1 teaspoon salt
2 tablespoons baking powder
4 teaspoons sugar
1 cup chopped toasted pecans
1 cup fresh or frozen corn kernels

1. In a large mixing bowl, combine the eggs, 2 cups milk, melted butter, and vanilla. In a separate bowl, combine the flour, salt, baking powder, and sugar, then add the pecans and corn. Mix the dry ingredients with the wet ones, stirring the batter with a large wooden spoon until well mixed. Cover tightly and refrigerate overnight.

The next day

2. If the batter seems too stiff, add more milk. (If you store the batter for several days, it will darken slightly on the top and the butter may separate slightly. Don't be concerned; just stir lightly and use.) Preheat a waffle iron and make waffles according to the manufacturer's instructions.

Breakfast Sausage Calzone

1830 Admiral's Quarters Inn
Boothbay Harbor, Maine
www.admiralsquartersinn.com

We almost always serve this sausage calzone along with our homemade oatmeal, and we save this dish for hearty snow mornings. Guests are now begging us to stop serving it in hopes it will stop snowing! We headline it as our Italian breakfast. It's a great dish for breakfast and dinner.

—DEB HALLSTROM, INNKEEPER

SERVES 12

2 loaves (1 pound each) frozen white bread dough, thawed

1 1/2 pounds bulk pork sausage

1/4 cup sliced fresh mushrooms

1/2 cup finely chopped onion

3 large eggs

2 1/2 cups shredded mozzarella cheese

1 teaspoon dried basil

1 teaspoon dried parsley flakes

1 teaspoon dried rosemary, crushed

1 teaspoon garlic powder or Adobo seasoning

Vegetable oil or nonstick vegetable oil spray

1. Allow the dough to rise in a warm place until doubled. Meanwhile, place a large skillet over medium heat and add the sausage. Fry the sausage, crumbling it, until lightly browned. Add the mushrooms and onion, and continue to fry until the sausage is well browned and the onions are tender. Transfer to paper towels to drain and allow to cool, then put in a mixing bowl.

2. Add 2 eggs and the mozzarella cheese to the cooled sausage mixture. Add basil, parsley, rosemary, and garlic powder and mix well.

3. Oil or spray a baking sheet and set aside. Roll each ball of dough into a 16 × 12-inch rectangle. Spread half the sausage mixture on each within 1 inch of the edge. Roll up, jelly-roll style, starting at the narrow end. Seal the edges. To allow for further rising, place on the baking sheet with several inches between the 2 rolls. Cover and refrigerate overnight.

The next day

4. Preheat the oven to 350°F. Bake the rolls until risen and light golden brown, about 25 minutes. Beat the remaining egg in a small bowl and brush over the loaves. Bake until the loaves are firm and brown, 5 to 10 minutes more. Serve warm.

Valley Farms' Baked Apples

Inn at Valley Farms Bed & Breakfast
Walpole, New Hampshire
www.innatvalleyfarms.com

Our 105-acre organic farm is bordered on two sides by a 500-acre orchard, which grows over sixty varieties of apples. Fall is one of our favorite times of the year to cook because of the local abundance of great produce. Every year, we get excited as we anticipate trying this recipe with new varieties of apples. Baking apples are best in this recipe, as they hold their shape better when cooked, but we've had success varying the cooking time and using a variety of our favorite eating apples. Fresh local honey and cider add a nice touch. This is a guest favorite and almost a meal in and of itself.

If you're in a hurry in the morning, you can speed the cooking time by partially cooking the apples and their liquid in a microwave and then finishing in the oven. If using the microwave, just be sure to turn the apples every few minutes of cooking so they cook evenly.

—JACQUELINE BADDERS, INNKEEPER

SERVES 8

8 large apples (Cortland, Gala, Winesap,
Fortune, Honey Crisp)

$^3/_4$ cup granola

$^2/_3$ cup raisins

$^2/_3$ cup chopped pecans or walnuts

$^3/_4$ teaspoon ground cinnamon

$^1/_4$ teaspoon grated nutmeg

10 tablespoons honey

6 tablespoons ($^3/_4$ stick) butter

3 tablespoons lemon juice

$1^1/_2$ cups apple cider (or substitute apple or
apple/cranberry juice)

Fresh mint leaves, for garnish

1. Core the apples and enlarge the hole slightly to leave room for the filling. Make several small slits in the sides of the apple skin.

2. In a small bowl, combine the granola, raisins, nuts, cinnamon, and nutmeg. Add 6 tablespoons of the honey. Pack the filling lightly into the apples and place them in a baking pan just large enough to fit the apples.

3. In a small saucepan, combine the remaining 4 tablespoons of honey with the butter, lemon juice, and cider. Place over medium heat and bring just to a boil. Cool the liquid a bit before pouring over the apples to prevent discoloration of the apple skin. Cover the pan with aluminum foil and refrigerate overnight.

The next day

4. Remove the pan from the refrigerator and allow to sit at room temperature for about 30 minutes. Preheat the oven to 350°F. Bake the apples, covered, for 15 minutes. Remove the cover, baste the apples, and continue baking until fork-tender, about 30 minutes, depending on the size and type of apple. Place the cooked apples in individual serving bowls, ladle with juice from the pan, and garnish with fresh mint.

Valley Farms' Baked Oatmeal

Inn at Valley Farms Bed & Breakfast
Walpole, New Hampshire
www.innatvalleyfarms.com

This recipe can be halved or easily modified with additions to suit your cupboard or your guests' needs.

SERVES 8 TO 10

5 cups rolled oats
³/4 cup raisins
³/4 cup chopped walnuts (optional)
2 apples, peeled, cored, and grated
1 tablespoon baking powder
1 teaspoon ground cinnamon
1 teaspoon pure vanilla extract
Dash of salt

2¹/₂ cups milk, plus additional for serving
4 large eggs, beaten
¹/₂ cup honey
Half-and-half, for serving
Maple syrup, for serving

1. In a large bowl, mix together the oats, raisins, walnuts (if using), and apples. Add the baking powder, cinnamon, vanilla, salt, 2¹/₂ cups milk, eggs, and honey. Mix well and pour into an ungreased 9 × 13-inch glass baking pan. Cover and refrigerate overnight.

The next day

2. Remove the pan from the refrigerator and allow to sit at room temperature for about 30 minutes. Preheat the oven to 350°F. Bake the oatmeal until lightly golden, about 30 to 40 minutes; do not overbake.

3. Portion into individual bowls and serve with milk or half-and-half and warm maple syrup.

Breakfast Bread Pudding

Historic Statesboro Inn and Restaurant
Statesboro, Georgia
www.statesboroinn.com

Puddings originated as a fourteenth-century "porridge" often made of cereals, bread crumbs, mutton, and beef with raisins, currants, and spices. While in Britain they are a favorite for Christmas and served mainly as a dessert, Americans have enjoyed flavorful bread puddings for all occasions. This dish also makes a delicious dessert served with hot vanilla sauce and a touch of cinnamon.

SERVES 10

Butter, for greasing the pan

One loaf of French, Italian, or challah bread

1½ cups dried or fresh fruit (raisins, apricots, cherries, cranberries, or fresh blueberries)

½ cup chopped walnuts or pecans, optional

1½ cups sugar

6 large eggs

1 teaspoon cinnamon

5 cups milk or half-and-half

2 tablespoons vanilla extract

1. Butter the bottom and sides of a 13 × 9 × 2-inch pan and cover the bottom with cubes of French, Italian, or challah bread. Sprinkle the top with dried or fresh fruits. Top with nuts, if desired.

2. In a medium bowl, combine sugar, eggs, cinnamon, milk, and vanilla; whisk to blend. Pour over the casserole and press down so all the bread is covered. Cover with plastic wrap and refrigerate overnight.

The next day

3. Bring the pan to room temperature. Preheat the oven to 350°F. Cover the pan with foil and bake covered for 45 minutes. Uncover and allow to brown for a few minutes. Cut and serve with a side of maple syrup or a dollop of sweetened sour cream.

Cranberry Nut Breakfast Rolls

Acworth Inn
Cummaquid, Massachusetts
www.acworthinn.com

Cape Cod is brimming with cranberries in the fall.
The bogs are beautiful when ready for harvest.
Enjoy them in this recipe.

MAKES 24 ROLLS

FOR THE ROLLS
$^1/_4$ cup orange juice
$^1/_3$ cup sweetened dried cranberries
$^1/_4$ cup ($^1/_2$ stick) butter, melted and cooled
1 cup buttermilk
2 large eggs

¾ cup granulated sugar

1 teaspoon salt

1 tablespoon active dry yeast

3 cups bread flour

⅓ cup coarsely chopped roasted pecans or walnuts

Vegetable oil or nonstick vegetable oil spray

6 tablespoons (¾ stick) butter, softened

Zest of 1 orange, removed in strips and finely diced

½ cup heavy cream (optional)

FOR THE ICING

2 cups confectioners' sugar

¼ teaspoon pure orange extract

¼ cup strained fresh orange juice, or as needed

1. For the rolls, bring the orange juice to a boil in a small saucepan and place it in a bowl with the dried cranberries. Let stand for 10 minutes, then strain, reserving the liquid. Gently heat the melted butter with the buttermilk until warm (not more than 115°F). Place in a mixing bowl. Add the eggs, ¼ cup granulated sugar, salt, and yeast and mix together. Add the flour and knead until the dough is cohesive. Add the strained cranberries and nuts and distribute evenly throughout the dough, then continue to knead until it is smooth and elastic.

2. Oil or spray a large mixing bowl. Shape the dough into a ball and place in the bowl, turning to coat with the oil. Cover with a damp cloth and let rise until double, about 1 hour.

3. Oil or spray two 9-inch cake pans and set aside. Divide the dough in half. Roll one half into a 12 × 8-inch rectangle. Smooth 3 tablespoons of the softened butter on the dough. Sprinkle with half the orange zest and ¼ cup of the granulated sugar. Roll up from the long side. Dampen the edge with water and seal the seam. Cut 12 even slices. Place the rolls, cut-side down, into a cake pan. Repeat with the remaining dough. Cover the pans and refrigerate overnight.

The next day

(rolls can be refrigerated up to 4 days)

4. Preheat the oven to 375°F. Remove the dough from the refrigerator and place in a warm place to rise until the rolls have doubled, about 30 minutes. For a creamier roll, drizzle ¼ cup heavy cream over each pan of rolls. Bake for 20 minutes, or until golden brown.

5. While the rolls are baking, prepare the icing. In a small bowl, combine the confectioners' sugar, orange extract, and orange juice. Whisk until smooth.

6. To ice the rolls, place the cooling rack over a tray or foil to catch any drips. Use a brush or spoon to spread a thin coat of icing over the tops of the rolls. Transfer the rolls to a plate and serve warm.

Chocolate Zucchini Muffins

Otters Pond Bed & Breakfast
Orcas Island, Washington
www.otterspond.com

My friend's garden tended to have too many zuc-
chinis, so they generously shared their bounty.
This muffin recipe works perfectly for an
overzealous zucchini crop. I shred the zucchini into
2-cup portions and freeze until needed. The
muffins taste like brownies!
—CARL & SUSAN SILVERNAIL, INNKEEPERS

SERVES 16

3 cups all-purpose flour (or gluten-free flour mix)
2 cups sugar
$^1/_3$ cup unsweetened cocoa powder
1 teaspoon baking soda
$^1/_2$ teaspoon baking powder
1 teaspoon salt
$^1/_2$ teaspoon ground cinnamon
$^1/_4$ teaspoon ground cloves
$^1/_4$ teaspoon grated nutmeg
3 large eggs, beaten
1 cup vegetable oil
$1^1/_2$ teaspoons pure vanilla extract
2 cups grated zucchini
$^1/_2$ cup chopped walnuts
$^1/_2$ cup semisweet chocolate chips
Nonstick vegetable oil spray

1. In a large bowl, combine the flour, sugar, cocoa pow-der, baking soda, baking powder, salt, cinnamon, cloves, and nutmeg. Whisk until blended. Add the eggs, oil, and vanilla and mix until well combined.

2. Add the zucchini, walnuts, and chocolate chips and mix again. Cover and refrigerate overnight.

The next day

3. Preheat the oven to 350°F. Spray 16 muffin cups or 32 mini-muffin cups, or line with paper inserts. Pour the bat-ter into the cups, filling each about two-thirds full. Bake mini-muffins for 12 minutes; standard muffins, 20 to 22 minutes.

Sugar Hill Inn Scones

Sugar Hill Inn
Sugar Hill, New Hampshire
www.sugarhillinn.com

Our inn is truly a work in progress. One morning
we were sitting on our deck with our guests
Arthur and Carole, enjoying these scones. Arthur,
a builder/contractor from upstate New York,
looked around our deck and had a vision of a new,
enlarged deck. He began to tell us his vision and
all of a sudden it became our vision too.
Before we knew it, Arthur was back,
building us a new deck!—C.G.

SERVES 8

2 cups cake flour

2 cups all-purpose flour, plus additional flour as needed

5 tablespoons sugar, plus more for dusting

$1^1/_2$ tablespoons baking soda

$1^1/_2$ tablespoons cream of tartar

1 teaspoon salt

$2^1/_2$ cups heavy cream

3 tablespoons milk to brush scones

1. Sift together the cake flour, 2 cups all-purpose flour, 5 tablespoons sugar, baking soda, cream of tartar, and salt. Sift two more times, then place in a mixing bowl.

2. Add the cream and stir until the mixture holds together. Turn onto a lightly floured surface and knead twelve times. Roll the dough to a ³/₄-inch thickness. Cut into the desired shapes (triangles, rounds, or squares), sized for individual portions. Cover tightly in plastic wrap and chill overnight.

The next day
3. Brush with milk and dust with sugar. Bake until lightly browned, 12 to 15 minutes. Serve warm.

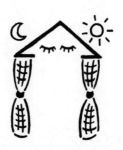

Brunch

Begin your brunch with our First Colony Juice Cordial (page 61). In addition, our Blueberry-Stuffed French Toast (page 45) has been hailed as the *very* best ever. Complement your brunch with our Bacon and Egg Lasagne (page 128). Brunch wouldn't be complete without Never-Fail Hash Browns (page 115). Toss in a few Tchoupitoulas (Chop-a-TOO-lus) Chicken Wings (page 25), and a fruit compote like our Hot Fruit Casserole (page 111), and you're sure to please. Dessert? Try the Chocolate Ladyfinger Cake (page 264). Delicious!

Decadent French Toast Soufflé

Foothill House
Calistoga, California
www.foothillhouse.com

Easy to make and oh, so good, this is one of our
favorite recipes served at our inn. —C.G.

SERVES 6

FOR THE FRENCH TOAST
Vegetable oil or nonstick vegetable oil spray
4 large or 5 medium croissants
6 ounces cream cheese, softened
1/2 cup (1 stick) butter, softened
3/4 cup maple syrup
10 large eggs
3 cups half-and-half
1 teaspoon ground cinnamon

FOR THE SAUCE
1/2 cup (1 stick) butter
1/2 cup maple syrup

FOR THE TOPPING
Chopped pecans
Confectioners' sugar
Edible flowers or berries, for garnish

1. For the French toast, oil or spray eight 1-cup soufflé
dishes or a 9 × 12-inch glass baking dish. In a food pro-

cessor, coarsely chop the croissants, then spread them evenly in the dish(es).

2. In a food processor, combine the cream cheese, butter, and $1/4$ cup of maple syrup. Dollop heaping tablespoons in the middle of the croissant pieces.

3. In a large bowl, beat the eggs, the remaining $1/2$ cup maple syrup, and the half-and-half. Pour over the mixture in the dish(es) and sprinkle with the cinnamon. Cover and refrigerate overnight.

The next day

4. Preheat the oven to 350°F. Uncover the French toast and bake until golden brown, 45 to 50 minutes.

5. For the sauce, heat the butter and maple syrup in a small saucepan, and pour over the warm soufflé.

6. For the topping, sprinkle with chopped pecans and confectioners' sugar. Garnish with edible flowers or berries.

Virginia Ham Tarts

The Trillium House
Wintergreen, Virginia
(The Trillium House is no longer in operation.)

Ham traditionally graces our Easter tables, often
glazed with honey and brown sugar, studded with
cloves, and garnished with pineapple or
apple rings. These tarts are perfect for
using up leftover ham.—C.G.

Uses 4 miniature muffin tins (12 compartments each)

Vegetable oil or nonstick vegetable oil spray
4 large sheets phyllo dough
4 tablespoons ($^1/_2$ stick) butter, melted
1 cup finely chopped Virginia ham
1 cup sharp cheese
$^3/_4$ cup shredded tart apple
$^1/_4$ cup finely crushed Ritz cracker crumbs

1. Oil or spray 48 miniature tart or muffin cups and set aside. Lay one sheet of phyllo on a large cutting board and brush generously with melted butter. Repeat with the second and third sheets, stacking the sheets as you go. Top with a fourth sheet, leaving it unbuttered.

2. Cut the layered phyllo into 48 layered $3^1/_2$- to 4-inch squares. Press into the tart or muffin tins.

3. In a medium mixing bowl, combine the ham, cheese, apple, and cracker crumbs; mix well. Press about 1 tablespoon of the mixture into each phyllo shell. Wrap and refrigerate overnight.

The next day

4. Preheat the oven to 350°F. Bake the tarts, uncovered, until golden brown, about 20 minutes. Serve warm.

Watch Hill Brie Strata with Fruit Salsa

Watch Hill Bed & Breakfast
Watch Hill, Rhode Island
(The Watch Hill Bed & Breakfast is no longer in operation.)

Here's a shortcut for the salsa: Use whatever ripe
fruit you have on hand and mix it with some
compatible jam. Mix in a small pan, simmering
until blended. Cool and serve at room temperature.
This recipe is always a favorite at the
Nantucket House.—C.G.

SERVES 8 TO 10

FOR THE FRUIT SALSA

1 pint fresh strawberries, diced
1 Anjou pear, cored and diced
1 red apple, cored and diced
1 tablespoon honey
1 tablespoon fresh lime juice

FOR THE STRATA

Vegetable oil or nonstick vegetable oil spray
4 tablespoons ($\frac{1}{2}$ stick) butter, softened
8 to 10 slices white bread, crusts removed
1 pound Brie cheese, rind removed, cut into $\frac{1}{2}$-inch cubes
4 large eggs
$1\frac{1}{2}$ cups milk
1 teaspoon salt
Paprika

1. For the fruit salsa, combine the strawberries, pear, apple, honey, and lime juice in a mixing bowl. Cover and refrigerate overnight.

2. For the strata, oil or spray a 9 × 12-inch glass baking pan. Butter both sides of the bread slices. Place half the bread slices into the baking pan and top with half the Brie cubes. Repeat with the remaining bread and Brie.

3. In a medium bowl, whisk the eggs together with the milk and salt. Pour the egg and milk mixture over the bread. Cover and refrigerate overnight.

The next day

4. Remove the fruit salsa from the refrigerator and allow to come to room temperature.

5. Remove the strata from the refrigerator 30 minutes before baking. Preheat the oven to 350°F. Sprinkle the strata with paprika and bake until the top is golden brown, 35 to 40 minutes. To serve, cut the strata into squares and top with the fruit salsa.

Casserole Florentine

Harbor House Inn
Hyannis, Massachusetts
www.harborhouseinn.net

A couple from New York came to us for a one-night
stay. They arrived around 6:00 P.M. Saturday and
left around 10:00 A.M. Sunday. Since their stay was
brief, we didn't have much chance to chat. After
they left, I went up to strip their room and, much to
my surprise, discovered that they had rearranged
most of the furniture! They did a good job—the
room remains that way today.—C.G.

SERVES 6 TO 8

---

1 pound bulk sausage

4 large eggs

$2^{1}/_{4}$ cups milk

1 can condensed cream of mushroom soup

1 package (10 ounces) frozen chopped spinach, thawed
and squeezed dry

$^{1}/_{4}$ pound fresh sliced mushrooms

1 cup (4 ounces) shredded sharp Cheddar cheese

1 cup (4 ounces) shredded Monterey Jack cheese

$^{1}/_{4}$ teaspoon dry mustard

Vegetable oil or nonstick vegetable oil spray

$2^{1}/_{2}$ cups seasoned croutons

Picante sauce or salsa, for serving

1. Crumble the sausage into a medium skillet and cook
over medium heat, stirring occasionally, until browned.
Drain off the drippings and set the sausage aside.

2. In a large bowl, whisk the eggs and milk until blended. Add the soup, spinach, mushrooms, cheeses, and mustard. Stir until well blended and set aside overnight.

3. Lightly oil or spray a 9 × 13-inch glass baking dish. Spread the croutons across the bottom of the dish. Top the croutons with the sausage and pour the egg mixture over all. Cover and refrigerate overnight.

The next day
4. Preheat the oven to 325°F. Bake the casserole, uncovered, until set and lightly browned on top, 50 to 55 minutes. Serve hot, with picante sauce or salsa.

Stuffed Egg Casserole

The Abbey
Cape May, New Jersey
www.abbeybedandbreakfast.com

The secret to hard-boiled eggs is to start the eggs
in a pan of cold water with a dash of salt. Heat to
boiling, then lower the heat to a simmer for 10 to 12
minutes. Drain the hot water off the eggs and
immediately immerse the eggs in cold water. Peel
the eggs under cold running water—
the shells will slide right off.

SERVES 6

FOR THE STUFFED EGGS
Butter, for greasing the dish

6 large eggs, hard-boiled and peeled

4 tablespoons (^{1}/$_2$ stick) butter, melted and cooled

^{1}/$_2$ teaspoon Worcestershire sauce

^{1}/$_4$ teaspoon dry mustard

1 can (2^1/$_2$ ounces) deviled ham

3 scallions, minced

FOR THE SAUCE
4 tablespoons (^{1}/$_2$ stick) butter

^{1}/$_4$ cup flour

2 cups milk

Salt and freshly ground black pepper

^{1}/$_2$ cup grated Swiss cheese

6 English muffins, toasted

1. Butter a 9 × 9-inch glass baking dish. Cut the eggs in half and remove the yolks. In a small bowl, mix the yolks with the melted butter, Worcestershire sauce, mustard, deviled ham, and scallions, blending until smooth.

2. Stuff the mixture into the egg-white halves. Arrange the eggs in the casserole dish.

3. For the sauce, melt the butter in a saucepan over low heat. Stir in the flour to form a paste and cook for a minute or two. Whisk in the milk and season to taste with salt and pepper. Heat until thickened. Pour the sauce over the eggs and sprinkle with the grated cheese. Cover and refrigerate overnight.

The next day

4. Preheat the oven to 350°F. Bake the casserole, uncovered, until the cheese has melted, 20 to 25 minutes. Serve over toasted English muffins.

Spiced Pear French Toast

The Heartstone Inn
Eureka Springs, Arkansas
www.heartstoneinn.com

You can substitute $1/4$ to $1/2$ cup brown sugar instead of the granulated sugar, cinnamon, and maple syrup. Also try adding sliced fresh strawberries for color in with the pears. It's delicious both ways. Garnish with pineapple and kiwi.

SERVES 6 TO 8

FOR THE FRENCH TOAST

Vegetable oil or nonstick vegetable oil spray

1 medium loaf cinnamon raisin bread, crusts removed

6 large eggs

$1/2$ cup sugar

$2^1/2$ cups milk

$1^1/2$ teaspoons pure vanilla extract

FOR THE SPICED PEARS

2 tablespoons ($1/4$ stick) butter

2 firm-ripe Anjou pears, cored and cut into chunks

1 teaspoon sugar

$1/2$ teaspoon ground cinnamon

Dash of grated nutmeg

$1/4$ cup maple syrup, plus additional for serving

1. For the French toast, oil or spray the sides and bottom of a 9 × 13-inch baking pan. Tear the bread into small pieces and scatter in the pan evenly.

2. In a small bowl, whisk the eggs and sugar until light. Add the milk and vanilla and whisk well. Pour over the bread evenly and press down with a spoon to make sure all the bread is submerged. Cover with foil, gently pressing down so the foil is right on the surface of the bread. Cover and refrigerate overnight.

The next day

3. Keeping the foil on the baking pan, slide the pan into a cold oven. Turn the oven to 350°F. After 25 minutes, remove the foil. Continue baking until the toast is puffed and golden, about 20 minutes. While the French toast is baking, prepare the spiced pears.

4. For the spiced pears, melt the butter in a nonstick frying pan over medium-high heat, then add the pears. Stir until the pears are well coated with butter, then sprinkle with the sugar, cinnamon, and nutmeg. Continue to cook until the pears begin to soften, about 3 minutes. Pour in $1/4$ cup maple syrup and cook until bubbly. Remove from the heat.

5. To serve, slice the French toast into 6 or 8 servings and top with the spiced pears. Serve with additional maple syrup, if desired.

Special Occasion
Cheese Blintz Casserole

Historic Statesboro Inn and Restaurant
Statesboro, Georgia
www.statesboroinn.com

This is a two-step process where you prepare a batter and a filling. Since both the batter and the filling are very liquid, it is best to use a shield on your mixer. To make a low-fat, low-sugar alternative, use low-fat sour cream, cream cheese, and cottage cheese. The equivalent amount of sugar substitute may be used instead of sugar. This filling is also great rolled into fluffy crepes and topped with reduced-sugar fruit topping.

SERVES 8 TO 10

FOR THE BATTER
Vegetable oil or nonstick vegetable oil spray
1 cup all-purpose flour
2 teaspoons baking powder
$1/2$ cup (1 stick) butter, softened
$1/2$ cup sugar
6 large eggs
$1/2$ cup orange juice
$1^1/2$ cups sour cream

FOR THE FILLING
8 ounces cream cheese, cut into 1-inch cubes
2 cups small-curd cottage cheese
2 tablespoons sugar

2 large eggs

1 teaspoon extract of your choice (see recipe)

FOR SERVING

Fresh berries or pitted or sliced fruit

1. For the batter, oil or spray a 9 × 13-inch glass baking pan. Sift the flour with the baking powder and set aside. In the bowl of an electric mixer, combine the butter, sugar, eggs, and orange juice. Add the flour mixture alternately with the sour cream, mixing well after each addition. Pour half of this over the bottom of the pan and set the other half aside while you make the filling.

2. For the filling, combine the cream cheese with the cottage cheese in the bowl of a mixer. Mix to blend. Add the sugar, eggs, and extract. (The type of extract may vary depending on the kind of fruit topping you use. Try vanilla extract with blueberry and strawberry, almond with cherry or peach.) Mix until well blended.

3. Using a ladle, pour the filling evenly over the blintz batter. Use a spatula to spread the filling out to the corners. Top the filling with the remaining blintz batter. Cover the casserole with foil and refrigerate overnight.

The next day

4. Bring the covered casserole to room temperature. Preheat the oven to 350°F. Bake, covered, until the casserole is puffy but firm, 50 to 60 minutes, removing the foil for the last 10 minutes of baking. Serve with the fresh fruit topping of your choice. Blueberries, pitted cherries, strawberries, and sliced peaches are all great.

Smoked Salmon Mold

Foothill House
Calistoga, California
www.foothillhouse.com

An e-mail reservation from a Disneyland employee
arrived. I replied that we'd love for her to visit us,
but I needed a new pair of mouse ears. She arrived
with a Minnie Mouse hat, complete with red ribbon
and my name printed on the back. The next day,
while serving this recipe, I wore my hat (my new
ears) and red polka-dot glasses! Certainly
a meal I'll always remember!

I prefer using a fish mold for this recipe; however, a
2-cup shallow oval dish also works well.
—DARLA ANDERSON, INNKEEPER

SERVES 10 TO 12

8 ounces cream cheese, at room temperature

1½ teaspoons butter, at room temperature

2 tablespoons finely chopped onion

8 ounces thinly sliced smoked salmon

½ small onion, thinly sliced

3 tablespoons capers

Fresh dill sprigs, for garnish

Mini-bagels, for serving

1. Line a 2-cup mold with plastic wrap. Combine the
cream cheese, butter, and chopped onion in a food processor. Line the mold with thinly sliced salmon encasing
the mold, leaving no gaps; set aside the remainder.

2. Spread half the cream cheese mixture in an uneven layer in the mold and sprinkle with about a third of the sliced onion and 1 tablespoon of the capers. Spread with the remaining cream cheese mixture, half the remaining smoked salmon, half the remaining sliced onion, and 1 tablespoon of the capers.

3. Top with the remaining smoked salmon. Completely cover the mold with plastic wrap and refrigerate overnight.

The next day

4. Invert the mold on a serving plate. Remove the plastic wrap and garnish the plate with the remaining sliced onion, tablespoon of capers, and dill sprigs. Serve with mini-bagels.

Smoked Haddock Leek and Gruyère Quiche

Blue Harbor House
Camden, Maine
www.blueharborhouse.com

We moved to Maine from owning a bed-and-breakfast in Edinburgh, Scotland. I love making American-style breakfasts; however, I have brought a few favorite recipes from Scotland, such as this one. Smoked haddock is not always easy to find, but it is well worth it when you do!
—ANNETTE & TERRY HAZZARD, INNKEEPERS

SERVES 8

1 pound smoked haddock (skinless, boneless smoked cod is a little easier to find)
$1^{1}/_{2}$ cups milk
1 tablespoon butter
2 medium leeks, well washed and thinly sliced
4 large eggs
$1^{1}/_{8}$ cups (about 3 ounces) shredded Gruyère cheese
Salt and freshly ground black pepper
1 pie shell (9 inches), partially baked until firm and lightly colored

1. In a medium saucepan, combine the haddock and milk. Place over medium-low heat and poach the fish until it flakes easily. Drain off the milk, allow the haddock to cool, then break into bite-sized pieces.

2. In a large skillet over medium-low heat, melt the butter. Add the leeks and cook until softened, about 2 minutes; set aside. In a large mixing bowl, beat the eggs until blended. Add the haddock and leeks and mix gently to blend. Cover and refrigerate overnight.

The next day

3. Preheat the oven to 350°F. Add 1 cup of the grated cheese to the fish mixture, and season to taste with salt and pepper. Gently spoon the mixture into the pie shell. Sprinkle with the remaining grated cheese. Bake, uncovered, until the filling is firm and the top is lightly golden, 35 to 45 minutes. (If the edges of the crust begin to brown too much, cover them with foil.) Allow to rest 5 minutes before serving.

Mushroom Celebration

Blowin A Gale Bed & Breakfast
Chatham, Massachusetts
(Blowin A Gale is no longer in operation.)

This is a great luncheon dish when
you have a crowd to feed.

SERVES 12 TO 14

5 cups (about 8 slices) cubed day-old bread

3 tablespoons butter, melted

2 tablespoons olive oil

1 pound mushrooms

^{1}/$_2$ cup diced celery

^{1}/$_2$ cup diced onions

^{1}/$_2$ cup diced peppers

^{1}/$_2$ cup mayonnaise

Salt and freshly ground black pepper

^{1}/$_2$ cup milk

2 large eggs

1 cup condensed cream of mushroom soup

1. Place the bread in a large bowl and drizzle with the melted butter; toss to combine. Spread about 2 cups of the bread cubes across the bottom of a 9 × 13-inch glass baking pan. Place a large skillet over medium heat and add the olive oil and mushrooms. Sauté until the mushrooms are tender. Remove from the heat and add the celery, onions, peppers, and mayonnaise. Season to taste with salt and pepper, then spread the mixture over the bread.

2. Top with 2 cups of bread cubes. In a small bowl, beat together the milk and eggs until blended, then pour over the casserole. Cover and refrigerate overnight.

The next day
3. Preheat the oven to 325°F. Pour the cream of mush-room soup over the casserole and top with the remaining 1 cup of bread cubes. Bake, uncovered, until browned, about 1 hour.

Seafood Brunch Strata

The Carriage House Inn
Chatham, Massachusetts
www.thecarriagehouseinn.com

Occasionally, in the kitchen we have what we refer to as coffee disasters. For example, if we start to brew a new pot of coffee with coffee already in the pot, we sometimes have an overflow situation. Generally guests have no idea when a coffee disaster is taking place, except for once. In a hurry, I brewed a second pot of coffee, only in my haste, I neglected to add coffee beans. My guests politely sipped their tinted water without comment until I realized my mistake, turned beet red, and apologized profusely. At least they loved the strata!
—JILL & JAMES MEYER, INNKEEPERS

SERVES 6 TO 9

Vegetable oil or nonstick vegetable oil spray

1 large loaf scali, challah, or other white specialty bread, crusts removed and discarded, cut into $^1/_2$- to $^3/_4$-inch dice

1 pound seafood salad or substitute (fresh lobster, shrimp, crabmeat mixed with 2 tablespoons mayonnaise)

$^1/_2$ cup slivered red onion

1 cup thinly sliced celery

$^1/_2$ cup thinly sliced red, orange, or yellow bell pepper

$1^1/_2$ cups shredded Swiss or Monterey Jack cheese

5 large eggs

3 cups milk

$^1/_4$ teaspoon dried mustard

Salt and freshly ground black pepper

1. Oil or spray an 11 × 13-inch glass casserole dish. Spread the diced bread evenly across the bottom. In a large bowl, mix together the seafood salad, red onion, celery, and bell pepper.

2. Spread the seafood-vegetable mixture evenly over the bread. Top with the cheese.

3. In a medium bowl, mix together the eggs, milk, and dried mustard. Season to taste with salt and pepper. Pour evenly over the casserole, cover, and refrigerate.

The next day

4. Preheat the oven to 350°F. Bake the strata, uncovered, until golden brown and bubbly, about 50 minutes. Cut into squares.

Hot Fruit Casserole

Inn at Riverbend
Pearlsburg, Virginia
www.innatriverbend.com

Whether your mode of relaxation is sleeping till noon, running five miles, or cooking up a storm, this recipe gives you ample relaxation time. It's great to use in winter as a first course or dessert and it keeps well for several days after baking.

SERVES 12

1 can (20 ounces) sliced pineapple, drained and cut into squares

1 can (15 ounces) sliced pears, drained

1 can (15 ounces) sliced peaches, drained

1 jar (15 ounces) apple rings, drained (optional)

1 stick butter

$1/2$ cup sugar

2 tablespoons flour

1 cup sherry

1. In a 9 × 13-inch glass baking dish, mix together the pineapple, pears, peaches, and apple rings (if using). In a double boiler or a heatproof bowl placed over (but not touching) simmering water, combine the butter, sugar, flour, and sherry. Heat, stirring, until the mixture becomes as thick as cream. Pour over the fruit, cover, and refrigerate overnight.

The next day

2. Preheat the oven to 350°F. Bake the casserole until thoroughly heated, about 30 minutes.

Christmas Cherries

The Governor's Inn
Ludlow, Vermont
www.thegovernorsinn.com

This is so pretty, it's great not only at Christmas but also for Valentine's Day.

SERVES 12

3 cans (1 pound each) pitted tart cherries, packed in water

2 cinnamon sticks

6 whole cloves

6 whole allspice

$1/2$ lemon

$1/2$ cup sugar

Pinch of salt

2 cups heavy cream

1 tablespoon all-purpose flour

2 cups Bordeaux wine

Sweetened whipped cream for garnish

1. Empty 2 cans of cherries and their juice into a large pot. Add the juice from the third can, but reserve the cherries. Add the cinnamon sticks, cloves, allspice, lemon, sugar, salt, and 1 cup of water. Bring to a boil, then reduce the heat to low.

2. Place the cream in a medium saucepan and heat just until steaming (do not boil). Whisk in the flour. Allow to cool slightly and add to the berry mixture. Add the wine and bring just to the boiling point. Strain and cool the mixture, discarding the boiled cherries. Add the reserved can of cherries, cover, and refrigerate for up to 2 weeks.

When ready to serve

3. To serve, place about 5 ounces of the mixture in a glass bowl or compote lined with crushed ice. Garnish with a dollop of whipped cream. Eat with soup spoons.

Hattie's Eggs

Nantucket House of Chatham Bed & Breakfast
Chatham, Massachusetts
www.chathaminn.com

Katherine, a friend of a friend, shares a traditional
dish from her mother-in-law, who often made this
dish for brunch. Now Katherine does the same. It's
a big hit at the Nantucket House as well.

SERVES 5

Vegetable oil or nonstick vegetable oil spray

5 slices Italian bread

1 1/2 cups chopped ham or little smokies

1 cup shredded Cheddar cheese

1 cup shredded Swiss cheese

5 large eggs

2 cups milk

1. Oil or spray a 9 × 9-inch glass baking pan. Spread the
bread across the bottom, overlapping slices if necessary.
Top with the ham and cheeses.

2. In a medium bowl, whisk together the eggs and milk.
Pour the egg mixture over the ham and cheese, cover, and
refrigerate overnight.

The next day

3. Preheat the oven to 325°F. Bake, uncovered, until
golden brown, about 1 hour.

Never~Fail
Hash Browns

Blowin A Gale Bed & Breakfast
Chatham, Massachusetts
(Blowin A Gale is no longer in operaation.)

This recipe is a great way to enhance any
breakfast or brunch entrée.

SERVES 6

2 pounds frozen diced hash browns

$^1/_2$ cup (1 stick) plus 2 tablespoons butter, melted

1 can condensed cream of mushroom or cream of
chicken soup

2 cups sour cream

2 cups grated cheese of your choice

$^1/_2$ teaspoon freshly ground black pepper

$^1/_2$ cup chopped onion

$^1/_2$ cup fresh bread crumbs

1. Spread the potatoes in a 9 × 12-inch glass casserole
dish and allow to thaw. In a large bowl, mix together $^1/_2$
cup of the melted butter, the soup, sour cream, cheese,
black pepper, and onion. Pour over the potatoes, cover,
and refrigerate overnight.

The next day

2. Preheat the oven to 350°F. In a mixing bowl, toss the
bread crumbs with 2 tablespoons of melted butter. Top
the casserole with the buttered bread crumbs. Bake until
golden brown, about 1 hour.

Miller House Grand Marnier French Toast

The William Miller House
Richmond, Virginia
www.ourfanhomes.com

We always serve fresh fruit. In the winter, it consists of oranges and grapefruits, so we often have large quantities of citrus rind. Since we don't want to waste the most flavorful part of the fruit, this recipe was born. The Grand Marnier was added after several trips to France and acquiring a good supply at a reasonable price!
—MIKE ROHDE, INNKEEPER

SERVES 4

6 large eggs
3/4 cup freshly squeezed orange juice
1/3 cup Grand Marnier
1/2 cup milk
3 tablespoons sugar
1/4 teaspoon pure vanilla extract
Pinch of salt
1 1/2 tablespoons finely grated orange zest
12 slices brioche or French bread, cut 3/4-inch thick
3 tablespoons butter, melted
Orange slices, for garnish
Confectioners' sugar
Maple syrup or other syrup, for serving

1. In a large bowl, beat the eggs just until smooth. Add the orange juice, Grand Marnier, milk, sugar, vanilla, salt, and orange zest and mix well.

2. Place the bread slices in a 9 × 13-inch glass pan, overlapping if necessary. Pour the egg mixture over all and turn several times. Cover and refrigerate overnight.

The next day

3. Preheat the oven to 400°F. Lightly brush a jelly roll pan or other rimmed baking pan with the melted butter. Place the bread slices on the pan and drizzle with any egg mixture that hasn't been soaked up by the bread. Bake until lightly browned, about 8 minutes. Turn and continue baking until browned on the other side.

Or melt the butter on a griddle or in a frying pan over medium-high heat. Place the bread slices on the griddle or in the pan and cook until lightly browned, 4 to 6 minutes. Turn and brown on the other side.

4. Arrange on a plate with the orange slices. Top with the confectioners' sugar and serve with syrup.

Eggs Benedict

Bedford Inn
Cape May, New Jersey
www.bedfordinn.com

This is the perfect brunch food. Legend has it that a
Wall Street financier named LeGrand Benedict,
a regular patron of Manhattan's Delmonico's
restaurant, complained that there was nothing new
on the menu. The chef's response was this dish.
Another myth credits the Delmonico's maître d'
and Mrs. Benedict with the recipe. Some say the
original base may have been toast instead of
English muffins. This version makes it super easy.

SERVES 8

4 English muffins, split and toasted

16 thin slices Canadian bacon

8 large eggs

2 tablespoons ($1/4$ stick) butter

2 tablespoons all-purpose flour

$1/2$ teaspoon paprika

$1/8$ teaspoon grated nutmeg

$1/8$ teaspoon freshly ground black pepper

1 cup milk

1 cup shredded Swiss cheese

$1/4$ cup dry white wine

1 tablespoon butter, melted

$1/2$ cup crushed cornflakes

1. In a 9 × 13-inch glass baking dish, arrange the muffins, cut-side up. Place 2 slices Canadian bacon on each muffin half.

2. Half fill a medium skillet with water and bring to a boil. Break 1 egg into a small bowl and carefully slide the egg into the boiling water. Repeat with 3 more eggs. Simmer, uncovered, until just set, about 3 minutes. Remove the eggs with a slotted spoon. Repeat with the remaining 4 eggs. Place 1 egg on top of each muffin half and set aside.

3. In a medium saucepan, melt 2 tablespoons butter. Stir in the flour, paprika, nutmeg, and pepper. Add the milk. Cook and stir until thickened and bubbly. Stir in the cheese, wine, and melted butter. Drizzle over the muffin stacks, cover, and refrigerate overnight.

The next day

4. Preheat the oven to 375°F. Sprinkle the muffin stacks with the crushed cornflakes. Bake, uncovered, until heated through, 20 to 25 minutes.

Easy Wild Rice Quiche

Franklin Victorian Bed & Breakfast
Sparta, Wisconsin
www.franklinvictorianbb.com

Do innkeepers ever burn the toast? You bet. We were into our second year of innkeeping, and I was preparing a breakfast spinach quiche for a full house of guests. Something just didn't work—maybe the spinach was too watery, too little cheese, I don't know. All I knew was that I had hungry people at the table and no particular entrée. My husband was just coming in from clamming and was met with tears and frustration. After I calmed down, I casually walked to the coffee shop across the street and bought one of every muffin and coffee cake they sold! The guests enjoyed their breakfast and, I'm happy to say, I've never had to do that again. Now I keep an extra supply of baked fruit/nut breads just in case!—C.G.

SERVES 6 TO 8

Vegetable oil or nonstick vegetable oil spray

6 large eggs

1 cup cooked wild rice, drained

1 can (10³/₄ ounces) condensed cream of mushroom soup

1¹/₂ cups shredded sharp Cheddar cheese

1 container (2.3 ounces) Hormel or Oscar Mayer bacon pieces or 5 to 6 tablespoons finely crumbled cooked bacon

1 tablespoon dry onion flakes

¹/₄ teaspoon salt

$^1/_4$ teaspoon freshly ground black pepper
Orange slices and mint leaves, for garnish

1. Oil or spray a 10-inch quiche pan and set aside. In a medium mixing bowl, beat the eggs until frothy.

2. Add the rice, soup, cheese, bacon bits, onion flakes, salt, and pepper. Mix only until blended; do not overmix. Pour into a quiche pan, cover, and refrigerate overnight.

The next day

3. Preheat the oven to 350°F. Bake the quiche, uncovered, until a knife inserted in the center comes out clean, 35 to 40 minutes. Let stand 5 to 10 minutes before serving. Garnish with the orange slices and mint leaves.

Cody Cowgirl Casserole

The Victorian Bed & Breakfast
Cody, Wyoming
www.codyguesthouses.com

Because Cody, Wyoming, is a true western town
and the home of Buffalo Bill, our guests have given
Wild West names to many of our favorite recipes.
This hearty recipe will give any cowboy or cowgirl a
good start to their day. For a shortcut, you can use
frozen hash browns with onions and peppers.
—WENDY EVARTS, PROPRIETOR

SERVES 6 TO 8

Vegetable oil or nonstick vegetable oil spray
1 pound bulk sausage, browned and drained
$^1/_2$ pound bacon, cooked and diced
12 ounces frozen hash browns or potatoes
1 medium green bell pepper, chopped
2 tablespoons chopped scallions
2 cups shredded Cheddar or Monterey Jack cheese
1 cup Bisquick
3 cups milk
$^1/_2$ teaspoon salt
4 large eggs

1. Oil or spray a 9 × 13-inch glass baking pan. In a large
bowl, combine the sausage, bacon, hash browns, bell pepper, scallions, and 1 cup of cheese. Spread in the baking
pan.

122 · Sleep On It

2. In another large bowl, whisk together the Bisquick, milk, salt, and eggs until blended. Pour over the potato mixture. Sprinkle with the remaining cup of cheese. Cover and refrigerate overnight (no longer than 24 hours).

The next day
3. Preheat the oven to 375°. Bake the casserole, uncovered, until light golden brown around the edges and the cheese is melted, 30 to 35 minutes. Let stand 10 minutes before serving.

Celebrations Inn
Veggie Egg Casserole

Celebrations Inn—Tea Time and Shoppes
Pomfret, Connecticut
www.celebrationsinn.com

This is what we served our very first guests. This has always been a favorite—it's colorful, and it offers a healthy dose of vegetables. Guests often request it for their return visits. I had a wife pull me aside to tell me that her husband will not eat broccoli at home with dinner, yet he ate every bite of this for breakfast! Have some fun playing with the ingredients; it's a very versatile recipe.
—JEAN BARTON, PROPRIETOR

SERVES 12

12 large eggs

4 cups milk

2 cups shredded Cheddar cheese

3 tablespoons crumbled Gorgonzola cheese

2 cups Bisquick

3 tablespoons Mrs. Dash regular seasoning blend

Dash of freshly ground black pepper

$4^1/2$ cups chopped broccoli

1 cup shredded carrots

1 cup shredded yellow squash

$^1/2$ cup slivered leeks, shallots, scallions, or onions
(or a mixture of all)

1 cup mixed finely shredded cheeses

1. In a large mixing bowl, combine the eggs, milk, and cheeses; mix well. Add the Bisquick, Mrs. Dash, black pepper, broccoli, carrots, squash, and leeks. Mix again until blended. Pour into a 12 × 18-inch pan. Cover and refrigerate overnight.

The next day

2. Preheat the oven to 350°F. Bake the casserole, uncovered, until the center is firm and lightly browned, about 30 to 40 minutes. Remove from the oven and sprinkle with about $^1/4$ cup mixed shredded cheese.

3. To serve, cut into 12 squares. Cut each square into a triangle. Sprinkle each plate with about 1 tablespoon shredded cheese and overlap one triangle slightly over the other to give some height.

Blueberry Crumb Cake

The Schramm House Bed & Breakfast
Burlington, Iowa
www.visitschramm.com

Have another slice—think of the blueberry's
antioxidant effect! This recipe is easy
and it's a crowd-pleaser.

SERVES 8

FOR THE CAKE
Nonstick vegetable oil spray
2 cups all-purpose flour
1 cup sugar
3 teaspoons baking powder
$1/4$ teaspoon salt
$1/2$ cup shortening
1 cup milk
2 large eggs, beaten
$1^{1}/_{2}$ cups fresh or frozen blueberries

FOR THE CRUMB TOPPING
1 cup sugar
$1/2$ cup all-purpose flour
$1/4$ cup ($1/2$ stick) butter, melted

1. Coat a 9 × 12-inch glass pan with nonstick spray and set aside. In a large mixing bowl, sift together the flour, sugar, baking powder, and salt. Using a pastry cutter or two knives, cut in the shortening.

2. In a small bowl, combine the milk and eggs. Beat until mixed and add to the dry ingredients. Mix lightly and fold in the berries. Spread in the pan, cover, and refrigerate overnight.

The next day

3. Preheat the oven to 375°F. For the crumb topping, combine the sugar, flour, and melted butter in a small bowl. Mix until crumbly and spread on top of the batter. Bake, uncovered, until a cake tester inserted into the center comes out clean and the topping is lightly browned, about 25 minutes. Cut into squares to serve.

Blintz Soufflé

Maytown Manor Bed & Breakfast
Maytown, Pennsylvania
www.maytownmanorbandb.com

The secret to a great soufflé is the egg whites. They
expand as they heat, producing the souffle's airy
texture. To get the best height, egg whites should
be at room temperature. Feel free to
add one or two more egg whites than
what the recipe calls for.

SERVES 6 TO 8

FOR THE BATTER
1/2 cup (1 stick) butter, softened
1/3 cup sugar
6 large eggs

1 1/2 cups sour cream
1/2 cup orange juice
1 cup all-purpose flour
2 teaspoons baking powder
Nonstick vegetable oil spray

FOR THE FILLING
8 ounces cream cheese, at room temperature
2 cups small-curd cottage cheese
2 large egg yolks
1 tablespoon sugar
1 teaspoon pure vanilla extract
Maple syrup, berry syrup, or sour cream, for serving

1. For the batter, combine the butter, sugar, eggs, sour cream, orange juice, flour, and baking powder in a large mixing bowl. Mix until smooth.

2. For the filling, combine the cream cheese, cottage cheese, egg yolks, sugar, and vanilla in a large mixing bowl. Mix until smooth.

3. Spray a 9 × 13-inch glass baking dish and spread half the batter in the pan. Drop the filling by spoonfuls over the batter, spreading it out as much as possible with a knife. The filling and batter will mix slightly. Pour the remaining batter on top, cover, and refrigerate overnight.

The next day

4. Preheat the oven to 350°F. Remove the pan from the refrigerator and allow to come to room temperature. Bake, uncovered, until puffed and golden brown, about 1 hour. Cut into serving portions. Serve with syrup or sour cream.

Bacon and Egg Lasagne

Fitzgerald's Irish Bed & Breakfast
Painesville, Ohio
www.fitzgeraldsbnb.com

In 1998, we bought our home and spent almost two years renovating it. We had no idea when we bought it that we would someday turn it into a bed-and-breakfast. So many people used to ask us if they could see the inside that one day my husband and I jokingly said, "Let's make it a bed-and-breakfast." To our surprise, it was already zoned for a business, and before long, we were opening our doors!—DEBRA & TOM FITZGERALD

SERVES 12

1 pound bacon, cut into 1-inch pieces

1 cup chopped onions

1/3 cup all-purpose flour

1/2 teaspoon salt

1/4 teaspoon freshly ground black pepper

4 cups milk

Vegetable oil or nonstick vegetable oil spray

12 lasagna noodles, cooked and drained

12 hard-boiled eggs, sliced

2 cups (8 ounces) shredded Swiss cheese

1/3 cup grated Parmesan cheese

2 tablespoons chopped parsley

1. In a large skillet, cook the bacon until crisp. Drain, reserving 1/3 cup of the fat from the pan. Set the bacon aside.

Cook the onions in the bacon drippings until tender. Add the flour, salt, and pepper; stir to make a paste. Add the milk; cook and stir until the mixture comes to a boil and is thickened.

2. Oil or spray a 9 × 13-inch glass baking pan. Spoon a small amount of the white sauce into the bottom of pan. Divide the lasagna noodles, bacon, white sauce, eggs, and Swiss cheese into thirds; layer in the pan. Sprinkle with the Parmesan cheese. Cover and refrigerate overnight.

The next day

3. Preheat the oven to 350°F. Bake the lasagne, covered, for 25 minutes. Uncover and bake 15 to 20 minutes longer, or until the lasagne is hot and the top is lightly browned. Garnish with the parsley and serve.

Apricot Cranberry Risotto

Two Sisters Inn, A Bed & Breakfast
Manitou Springs, Colorado
www.twosisinn.com

At Two Sisters Inn, we have a tradition of always serving a completely different breakfast to our returning guests. This Apricot Cranberry Risotto recipe was inspired by one of our repeat guests from Kansas who is a soybean farmer and Grange manager. Because he's always around soy, he said he never wanted to see another soy product in his life. Teasingly, we bet him that we could serve him a delicious soy dish and he would never know it, so the challenge was on! Voilà! Apricot Cranberry Risotto was created and added to our permanent repertoire. Now when he visits, he doesn't know which day a soy recipe will be served, but he knows that one of the dishes will have soy in it!

—WENDY GOLDSTEIN & SHARON SMITH, INNKEEPERS

SERVES 6

1 cup fat-free or soy milk

2 cups vanilla soy milk

$1/3$ cup light brown sugar

$1/3$ cup arborio rice

1 cinnamon stick

$1/8$ teaspoon grated nutmeg

$1/2$ cup chopped dried apricots

$1/2$ cup chopped dried cranberries

Raspberries and mint leaves, for garnish

1. In a heavy saucepan, combine the milks, brown sugar, rice, cinnamon stick, and nutmeg. Place over medium-low heat and bring to a boil, watching carefully that it does not boil up and overflow. Reduce the heat to as low as possible and cover. Simmer until the rice is done, about 30 minutes.

2. Stir in the apricots and cranberries and cook for several minutes, until the fruit is slightly softened. Remove from the heat and pour into six ¹/₂-cup ramekins. Let cool for 15 minutes, then cover and refrigerate overnight to allow the mixture to thicken.

The next day

3. Place the ramekins in a microwave or low oven to warm slightly before serving. Garnish with the raspberries and mint leaves.

Savory Artichoke Potato with Rosemary

The Huckleberry Inn
Warren, Connecticut
www.thehuckleberryinn.com

Some of my favorite recipes are ones I prepare the night before. They are delicious and I am so much more relaxed in the morning. You can bake this in a larger baking dish and cut into squares to serve. This is a very satisfying dish for your vegetarian guests if you simply omit the sausage.
—ANDREA DIMAURE, INNKEEPER

SERVES 4

Butter, for greasing the baking dish(es)

3 large red potatoes, boiled, cooled, and cut into bite-sized chunks

$3/4$ cup crumbled feta cheese

$1/4$ pound breakfast sausage, cooked, cooled, and crumbled

1 can (8 ounces) artichoke quarters, drained

1 roasted red pepper (home roasted and peeled, or bottled), cut into $1/2$-inch strips

1 tablespoon finely minced fresh rosemary, plus 1 decorative sprig for each serving dish

5 large eggs

1 cup half-and-half

Salt and freshly ground black pepper

1. Butter four 1-cup ramekins or one 8-inch square baking dish. In each dish, spread the potato chunks evenly and top with the crumbled cheese and sausage. Set 3 artichoke quarters in a triangular pattern on top. Arrange a roasted red pepper strip between the artichokes and sprinkle with the rosemary. Cover and refrigerate overnight.

The next day

2. Preheat the oven to 375°F. In a small bowl, whisk together the eggs and half-and-half. Uncover the casseroles and pour the custard gently over the vegetables; the dish(es) should be only two-thirds full since the eggs will expand when they bake.

3. Bake for approximately 15 minutes, or until puffed and golden brown. Season to taste with salt and pepper and garnish with a rosemary sprig.

Pineapple French Toast with Ambrosia Salsa

Rosewood Country Inn
Bradford, New Hampshire
www.rosewoodcountryinn.com

We first served this at our annual Mother and Daughter Weekend. This seemed like the perfect Sunday brunch entrée and it got rave reviews from everyone!—LESLEY MARQUIS, INNKEEPER

SERVES 6

1 can (20 ounces) pineapple chunks, in juice

$^1/_4$ cup toasted flaked coconut

4 tablespoons sugar

1 small loaf (10 ounces) French or Italian bread

3 large eggs

$1^1/_2$ cups milk

1 teaspoon pure vanilla extract

$^1/_4$ teaspoon salt

1 tablespoon butter

1 cup halved fresh strawberries

1 can (11 ounces) mandarin orange sections

Confectioners' sugar, for garnish

1. Drain the pineapple, reserving $^1/_4$ cup of juice. Place a small skillet over medium heat and add the coconut. Toss constantly until the coconut is lightly browned, then transfer to a plate to cool.

2. For the ambrosia salsa, in a medium bowl, combine the drained pineapple, coconut, and 2 tablespoons sugar. Cover and refrigerate until ready to serve.

3. For the French toast, cut the bread in ³/₄-inch-thick slices. In a 10 × 15-inch glass baking pan, arrange the bread slices in a single layer and set aside. In a large bowl, beat the eggs, milk, vanilla, salt, remaining 2 tablespoons sugar, and reserved pineapple juice. Mix until well blended. Pour over the bread, turning the slices to coat evenly. Cover and refrigerate overnight.

The next day

4. Melt the butter in a large skillet over medium heat. Add the bread, a few pieces at a time, and cook until browned on both sides, turning the bread once and adding more butter if necessary. To serve, stir the strawberries and orange sections into the salsa and spoon onto the French toast. Garnish with a sprinkling of confectioners' sugar.

Dinner

After working all day, simple recipes are a pleasure. Seafood au Gratin (page 220) is hearty and delicious. Prizewinning Pearson's Pond Healthy Ham Quiche (page 212) is quick to fix and perfect for leftovers the next day. For a meatless entrée, try the Southwestern Frittata (page 162). Sweet-and-Sour Carrots (page 156) are a nice addition to any meal, especially in the summer.

Shrimp-Stuffed Brioche

Grant Corner Inn
Santa Fe, New Mexico
www.grantcornerinn.com

We love to share our memories—here's a special
one. When I was growing up, my mother had what
we called the back closet, a room about 20 × 20 feet,
where she stored her specialties for
celebration : party hats of all sorts, balloons, doilies,
decorations, wrapping, and gifts galore. My mother
never forgot any occasion. All the hotel guests,
friends, and family, all birthdays, anniversaries,
births, and marriages were lovingly acknowledged.
And we loved her special attention. So at Grant
Corner Inn, we love a celebration ; it's our way of
giving a little sparkle to others ! You don't have to
wait for a special occasion to make these
wonderful Shrimp-Stuffed Brioche—they make
any dinner special.—LOUISE STEWART, INNKEEPER

SERVES 10

FOR THE PASTRY

1 package active dry yeast

$^1/_2$ cup warm water (110 to 115°F)

1 tablespoon sugar

2 tablespoons nonfat dry milk

1 teaspoon salt

2 to 2$^1/_4$ cups all-purpose flour

$^1/_2$ cup (1 stick) softened butter, plus additional for
greasing the muffin cups

3 large eggs

FOR THE GLAZE

1 egg yolk

1 tablespoon milk

FOR THE TARRAGON SHRIMP

1 pound raw medium shrimp, with shells

$^1/_2$ lemon

1 parsley sprig

6 peppercorns

$1^1/_2$ sticks unsalted butter

2 scallions, finely chopped

$^3/_4$ cup all-purpose flour

1 cup milk

2 cups half-and-half

2 tablespoons sherry

1 teaspoon dried tarragon

Salt

Freshly ground white pepper

Paprika

1. To make the pastry, combine the yeast, water, and sugar in the bowl of a heavy-duty electric mixer. Let stand 10 minutes, or until the mixture looks slightly foamy. Add the milk, salt, and 1 cup of flour and beat on medium-high speed for 3 minutes. Add $^1/_2$ cup of butter and beat for 2 more minutes. Turn the mixer down to medium speed, and alternately add the eggs and just enough flour to make a cohesive dough, adding the flour a half cup at a time and scraping the bowl frequently. Once all the ingredients have been added, beat the dough on medium speed for about 10 more minutes. The dough will be very sticky and elastic; most of it will be sticking to the beater.

2. Scrape the dough into a mixing bowl and cover with plastic wrap. Let sit in a warm spot until doubled, about $1^1/_2$ to 2 hours.

3. Punch the dough down, cover again, and refrigerate overnight.

The next day

4. Remove from the refrigerator and, using buttered hands, form the dough into a long, narrow roll. Cut the dough into 10 pieces. Grease well 10 cups of a 12-cup muffin tin. Taking one piece of dough, begin to pull out a part of dough about the size of a large marble. Continue pulling to the point where the smaller piece (which will become the topknot) is almost separated from the body of the brioche. Twisting the topknot and using your fingers to form a depression below, seat the smaller piece on top of and slightly inside of the body of the brioche. Repeat with all the dough pieces. Put each piece in a muffin cup and let sit in a warm spot until doubled.

5. Preheat the oven to 400°F. In a small bowl, beat the egg yolk with milk for the glaze. Brush on the brioche tops and bake until golden brown, 18 to 20 minutes. Slice off the topknot and hollow out the brioche a bit, pinching out bits of the baked dough with your fingers. Set aside and make the tarragon shrimp.

6. Shell and devein the shrimp, reserving the shells and tails. Put the shells and tails in a small saucepan and add 2 cups water, the lemon, parsley, and peppercorns. Cover and bring to a boil; simmer 30 minutes. Strain 1 cup of the shrimp stock into a small bowl and reserve.

7. In a medium saucepan, melt all but 2 tablespoons of the butter. Add the scallions and sauté until transparent. Add the flour, stirring to blend; cook 3 minutes on low heat. Gradually add the milk, then the half-and-half and reserved shrimp stock, stirring to incorporate. Add the sherry, cover, and set aside.

8. In a medium sauté pan, melt the remaining 2 tablespoons of butter. Add the shrimp and sauté until they curl and appear opaque, no more than 5 minutes. Add the tarragon. Combine the shrimp and sauce, and season to taste with salt, white pepper, and paprika.

9. To serve, place the hollowed-out brioches on small plates and fill with warm tarragon shrimp. Serve immediately. This recipe can be served as a brunch entrée or a main course. If using as a main course, a first course of soup in addition to a salad works nicely.

Teriyaki Roast Tenderloin

The Ballastone Inn
Savannah, Georgia
www.ballastone.com

The morning began like any other, with guests having breakfast and talking among themselves. I excused myself and went on my daily trek to the supermarket. Coming home, I heard the sirens. Driving down our street, I saw the blinking lights. Driving into our driveway, I saw our guests in bathrobes standing in the front yard under the tree away from the inn. Apparently, while I was at the supermarket, our smoke alarms had gone off and alerted the police and fire departments. After an extensive search, it was determined, much to everyone's relief, that a small spider had crawled into the smoke detector and set off the alarm. That called for another round of coffee and muffins so that everyone had a chance to relate their take on the morning's events.—C.G.

SERVES 6 TO 8

$^1/_2$ cup dry sherry

$^1/_4$ cup soy sauce

2 tablespoons dry onion soup mix

2 tablespoons brown sugar

$3^1/_2$ pounds whole filet of beef tenderloin

1 bunch watercress, for garnish (optional)

6 to 8 kumquats, for garnish (optional)

1. In a bowl just large enough to hold the tenderloin, combine the sherry, soy sauce, onion soup mix, and brown sugar. Add the tenderloin and turn to coat. Cover and refrigerate overnight.

The next day

2. Preheat the oven to 425°F. Place the meat in a roasting pan and roast 45 to 50 minutes, basting with half of the marinade. In a small saucepan, heat the remaining marinade and 2 tablespoons water until the mixture boils. Cut the meat into ¼-inch slices, arrange on a plate, and spoon the sauce over the meat. If desired, garnish with the watercress and kumquats.

Lamb Gourmet

The Governor's Inn
Ludlow, Vermont
www.thegovernorsinn.com

We had guests staying in our downstairs room—the Chatham Room. In this case, the guests did not lock their room. Our dog, Samantha, is *never* allowed in the guest rooms. However, on this particular evening, the guests were out and we were out and Samantha pushed open the door and proceeded to make herself comfortable on their bed. The guests arrived home before us and were surprised as well as shocked to find our 105-pound dog on their bed!! We came home shortly thereafter and were mortified. We apologized profusely, changed the bed linens, and promptly gave them a free night's stay!

We have a rather large feathered rooster on our reading table in the common room. Two days later as I was bringing breakfast to the table, next to this rooster was an exact smaller replica. It was as if the rooster had given birth! As I was quizzing all the guests as to who gave us the rooster, the guests from the Chatham Room burst out laughing. They said they wanted us to know that they had a sense of humor. They promised that their smaller rooster would be better behaved than Samantha!—C.G.

SERVES 16

1 bottle (750 ml) dry red wine
2 teaspoons minced fresh rosemary
6 tablespoons chopped shallots

2 celery stalks, chopped
2 carrots, peeled and grated
$1/2$ teaspoon freshly ground black pepper
4 garlic cloves, peeled and minced
$1/2$ cup loosely packed chopped parsley
16 loin lamb chops (about 3 to 4 ounces each)
1 cup veal stock or beef broth
$1/2$ cup (1 stick) butter
$1/4$ cup olive oil

1. In a medium saucepan, combine the wine, rosemary, shallots, celery, carrots, pepper, garlic, and parsley. Bring to a boil, reduce the heat, and simmer 20 minutes. Remove from the heat and allow to cool.

2. Place the lamb chops in a flat, shallow glass baking dish and pour the cooled marinade over them. Cover and refrigerate for 3 days, turning the chops over once during the marinating period.

After 3 days

3. Remove the lamb, strain the liquid, and boil it down to 1 cup. Add the veal stock and continue to boil until the liquid is reduced to 3 tablespoons. Remove from the heat and slowly whisk in the butter, 1 tablespoon at a time, to make a sauce. Set aside and keep warm.

4. Place a large heavy skillet over medium-high heat and add the olive oil. When the oil is shimmering, add the lamb chops and sauté, turning often, until browned and cooked to taste. To serve, spoon a pool of sauce on each warmed dinner plate and top with a chop.

Wild Rice Asparagus Quiche

The King's Cottage, A Bed & Breakfast
Lancaster, Pennsylvania
www.kingscottagebb.com

Sometimes our guests send us little presents that symbolize the state they live in or a longtime family recipe. One couple from Maryland sent us the ingredients for buckwheat pancakes, complete with the flour and syrup. Another couple from Minnesota sent us wild rice and a cookbook of wild rice recipes. It's fun to try these recipes, modify them a little to suit our taste, and create everlasting memories of our guests.

Try using the small mini-quiche pans to cook the quiches, then freeze and reheat as needed.—C.G.

SERVES 6

Vegetable oil

6 large eggs

1 1/2 cups cooked wild rice pilaf

1 package (10 ounces) frozen asparagus, thawed and chopped

1/2 cup skim or Lactaid milk

1/2 cup reduced-fat mayonnaise

2 tablespoons lemon juice

3/4 teaspoon dried dill

2 tablespoons crumbled blue cheese

1. Oil a 9-inch quiche pan or pie plate and set aside. In a medium bowl, beat 1 egg. Stir in the wild rice until well blended. Press the rice mixture onto the bottom and up the sides of the pan. Spoon the asparagus onto the bottom of the crust. Cover and refrigerate overnight.

The next day

2. Preheat the oven to 350°F. In a mixing bowl, beat together 5 eggs, the milk, mayonnaise, lemon juice, and dill until well blended. Pour the egg mixture into the prepared crust and sprinkle the blue cheese over the egg mixture.

3. Bake the quiche until puffed in the center and a knife inserted in the center comes out clean, about 35 to 40 minutes. Let stand 5 minutes before serving.

Veal with Peppers and Mushrooms

Nantucket House of Chatham Bed & Breakfast
South Chatham, Massachusetts
www.chathaminn.com

When shopping for Cubanelle peppers, look for the thin, misshapen green peppers usually found right next to the other sweet peppers.

SERVES 6

$^1/_4$ cup vegetable oil

2 pounds veal scaloppine, gently pounded until thin

2 large eggs, beaten

Italian-flavored bread crumbs

10 sweet Italian peppers, jarred,
or 10 fresh Cubanelle peppers

8 ounces sliced fresh mushrooms

1 cup sauterne or sherry

1 teaspoon salt

1. Place a large skillet over medium heat and add the oil. Dip the veal slices in the beaten eggs and then in the bread crumbs. Place in the skillet and fry until golden brown. Arrange in a 9 × 13-inch baking dish.

2. Return the skillet to medium heat and add the peppers. Sauté until softened. Place the peppers on top of the veal slices. Sauté the mushrooms in the same pan, and add to the veal and peppers.

3. Scrape the pan with a wooden spoon to dislodge any bits and pieces. Add the wine, $^1/_2$ cup water, and salt and stir for 1 minute. Pour the sauce over the veal, cover, and refrigerate overnight.

The next day

4. Preheat the oven to 350°F. Cover the pan with foil and bake for 45 minutes. Serve hot.

The Most Amazing Brisket Ever

Nantucket House of Chatham Bed & Breakfast
South Chatham, Massachusetts
www.chathaminn.com

This recipe has been met with rave reviews at many family holidays and special occasions. The spices create a heartwarming aroma in the house as the brisket simmers. Try using a roasting bag to preserve the juices, then pour the juices over garlic mashed potatoes.

SERVES 4

1 packet onion soup mix
1 cup ketchup
$^{1}/_{2}$ cup cider vinegar
$^{1}/_{2}$ cup brown sugar
Garlic powder
6 pounds beef brisket
Red wine, as needed

1. Preheat a broiler. In a shallow glass pan large enough to hold the brisket, combine the soup mix, ketchup, cider vinegar, brown sugar, and garlic powder to taste.

2. Brown the brisket on both sides under the broiler. Place the brisket in the pan of seasonings, and turn to coat well. Cover and refrigerate overnight.

The next day

3. Preheat the oven to 350°F. Cover the brisket with foil and bake, basting occasionally, for $2^{1}/_{2}$ hours.

4. To serve the brisket, cut into thin slices and place on a platter; keep warm. To make gravy, add red wine to taste in the roasting pan and stir the bottom with a wooden spoon to incorporate the cooked residue. Pour into a gravy boat and pass separately.

Tablespoon Bread

Sugar Hill Inn
Sugar Hill, New Hampshire
www.sugarhillinn.com

This recipe is very forgiving. We change it from
day to day. Our guests love the bread and
our waitstaff has to warn them not to fill up
on it so they can save room for dinner.
—JUDY & ORLO COOTS, INNKEEPERS

MAKES 2 BREAD STICKS OR 1 LARGE LOAF

3 cups all-purpose flour

1 tablespoon yeast

1 1/2 teaspoons salt

1 tablespoon butter, plus additional for greasing the bowl

1 tablespoon sugar

1 cup lukewarm water (about 105 to 110°F)

Cornmeal

1 large egg

Toppings for bread (salt, freshly ground black pepper,
poppy seed, sesame seed)

Variations

Herb Bread: Substitute 1 tablespoon oil for the butter.
Add 1 tablespoon chopped herbs of your choice to
the dough. Use a plastic blade if the herbs are already
chopped.

Salt Bread: Sprinkle the top liberally with salt.

Pepper Bread: Add 1 tablespoon freshly ground pepper
to the dough; sprinkle the top with 1 teaspoon more.

Garlic Bread: Add 1 tablespoon chopped garlic to the dough; process well to distribute.

1. In a food processor, combine 2 cups of flour, the yeast, salt, 1 tablespoon butter, and the sugar. Process to mix and slowly add ²/₃ cup lukewarm water until the dough comes together. Add the remaining cup of flour. Slowly add another ¹/₃ cup water until the dough comes together again.

2. Knead the dough by hand for a minute, then put into a bowl lightly greased with butter. Cover and place in a warm place until doubled in size, about 1 hour. Punch down the dough and if desired, divide into 2 pieces. Roll into the desired shape, cover, and refrigerate overnight.

The next day

3. Put the bread dough in or on a pan lightly coated with cornmeal. Beat the egg and then brush it on the dough and sprinkle on the desired topping. Place in a warm place until doubled in size, about 1 hour.

4. Preheat the oven to 350°F. Bake in the middle of the oven for 20 minutes, spin the bread around halfway, and cook 15 more minutes. If cooking 1 loaf, continue baking for 20 minutes. The bread should be a nice golden brown.

Spanish Omelette
(*Tortilla de Patatas*)

Tulip Tree Inn Bed & Breakfast
Angola, Indiana
www.tuliptree.com

We became acquainted with this dish while visiting our son and his family in Barcelona. *Tortilla de Patatas* is the national dish of Barcelona. Spanish women take great pride in tailoring this dish to their families' preference. Don't look for tortillas in the recipe because there aren't any! The true style in making the *Tortilla de Patatas* is to follow the recipe below. When the omelette is reasonably cooked on the bottom (firm on top), place an inverted plate on top of the frying pan and flip the omelette onto the plate. Then slide the omelette back into the frying pan and cook until firm. Serve at room temperature.
—KATY & MAC FRIEDLANDER, INNKEEPERS

SERVES 6 TO 8

6 tablespoons olive oil
1 onion, peeled and thinly sliced
1 pound potatoes, peeled and thinly sliced
12 large eggs
Salt

1. Place a large covered skillet with a heatproof handle over medium-low heat and add the oil. Arrange a layer of onions in the pan, topped by a layer of potatoes. Cover the skillet and cook the potatoes and onions until they are soft but not browned. Remove from the heat and set aside.

2. Preheat a broiler. In a large bowl, beat the eggs until smooth. Add a pinch of salt and gently mix in the cooked potatoes and onions. Return the mixture to the sauté pan and cook over medium-low heat until the eggs are cooked on the bottom but very loose on top. Place the pan under the broiler and brown the top; do not let it set completely. Cover and refrigerate overnight.

The next day

3. Place the omelette in the microwave at a low temperature for just a minute or two (or reheat in a low oven). Let the omelette rest for 10 minutes before removing it from the pan. Cut into slices and serve.

Sweet-and-Sour Carrots

Blowin A Gale Bed & Breakfast
Chatham, Massachusetts
(Blowin A Gale is no longer in operation.)

Did you know carrots originally had purple
exteriors and yellow flesh? It is said that in the
Middle Ages the Dutch developed the bright
orange carrot. The Irish and English make a carrot
pudding, the French make a sweet carrot stew, and
early New Englanders gave carrot cookies as
Christmas gifts. Holtville, California, dubs itself
"The Carrot Capital of the World."

SERVES 12

2 pounds carrots, peeled and diced
1 can condensed tomato soup
$3/4$ cup sugar
$1/2$ cup vegetable oil
$1/4$ cup red or white wine vinegar
1 green bell pepper, cored and diced
3 small onions, peeled and thinly sliced
1 teaspoon yellow mustard
1 teaspoon salt

1. Place the diced carrots in a medium saucepan and add
2 cups water. Cook over medium-low heat until the carrots are tender but not soft; they should still be firm.
Drain and allow to cool.

2. In a large mixing bowl, combine the soup, sugar, vegetable oil, vinegar, bell pepper, onions, and mustard. Mix well and season to taste with salt. Add the carrots and mix again. Cover and refrigerate overnight.

The next day

3. Serve cold, or place in a saucepan and reheat gently over low heat.

Sweet Potato Casserole

55 East Bed & Breakfast
Annapolis, Maryland
www.55east.com

This is wonderful with turkey or ham,
green beans, and corn bread.

SERVES 8

Vegetable oil or nonstick vegetable oil spray
3 pounds canned sweet potatoes, drained
$1^3/_4$ teaspoons salt
$^1/_2$ teaspoon finely grated lemon zest
1 teaspoon grated orange zest
$^1/_2$ cup orange juice
$^1/_3$ cup dark or light brown sugar
$^1/_3$ cup butter, softened

FOR THE TOPPING (OPTIONAL)
$^3/_4$ cup chopped pecans
$^1/_4$ cup dark or light brown sugar
3 tablespoons butter, melted

1. Oil or spray a 6-cup casserole dish and set aside. In a large mixing bowl, combine the sweet potatoes, salt, lemon and orange zests, orange juice, $^1/_3$ cup brown sugar, and $^1/_3$ cup softened butter.

2. Using a potato masher, mash to make a smooth puree. Spread the mixture evenly in the baking pan. For the topping (optional), in a small bowl combine the pecans, $^1/_4$ cup brown sugar, and 3 tablespoons melted butter. Spread the mixture over the mashed sweet potatoes in the baking pan. Cover with plastic wrap so that the wrap touches the entire surface of the top of the potatoes. Refrigerate overnight.

The next day
3. Remove the dish from the refrigerator 1 hour before baking. Preheat the oven to 375°F. Bake, uncovered, until the top begins to brown, about 1 hour.

Sunday Night Supper

Nantucket House of Chatham Bed & Breakfast
South Chatham, Massachusetts
www.chathaminn.com

Ever wonder how to slice an onion? Try this: Trim off both ends of the onion. Turn the onion onto the cut end and slice in half. Peel each half, place cut-side down, and slice with the grain.

Sunday dinner has always been special. This recipe is a throwback to simpler times and one that my grandmother made many Sunday nights. Gather the family and enjoy!—C.G.

SERVES 6

Vegetable oil or nonstick vegetable oil spray
2 tablespoons butter
1 pound mushrooms, sliced

3 medium onions, peeled and sliced
2 garlic cloves, peeled and minced
2 pounds boneless sirloin, cut into 1-inch cubes
$^1/_2$ cup red wine
2 cups beef broth
3 tablespoons soy sauce
3 tablespoons cornstarch
Mashed potatoes or noodles, for serving (optional)

1. Oil or spray a 10 × 10-inch glass baking dish. In a large skillet over medium heat, melt the butter. Add the mushrooms, onions, and garlic and sauté until the onions are translucent. With a slotted spoon, transfer to the baking dish.

2. Return the unwashed skillet to medium heat and add the sirloin cubes. Sauté until browned and add to the baking dish. Return the skillet to medium heat and add the wine, beef broth, soy sauce, and $2^1/_2$ cups water. Stir in the cornstarch, scraping the bottom of the pan. Stir until thickened, then pour into the casserole. Cover and chill overnight.

The next day

3. Preheat the oven to 325°F. Bake the casserole, uncovered, for 2 hours. If desired, serve over mashed potatoes or noodles.

Spicy BBQ Shrimp

Nantucket House of Chatham Bed & Breakfast
South Chatham, Massachusetts
www.chathaminn.com

In this recipe, the shrimp gets infused with flavor,
which seems hard to do with most marinades.
Serious shrimpers will polish
these off in no time!

SERVES 6

1 cup olive oil

Juice of 1 lemon

2 tablespoons hot pepper sauce

3 garlic cloves, peeled and minced

1 tablespoon tomato paste or ketchup

2 teaspoons dried oregano

1 teaspoon salt

1 teaspoon freshly ground black pepper

$1/4$ cup chopped fresh cilantro leaves

Super-hot sauce or chili powder, to taste (optional)

2 pounds large shrimp, shelled

Cooked rice or pasta, for serving (optional)

1. In a large bowl, mix together all of the ingredients except the shrimp and rice or pasta. Cover and allow to sit at
room temperature for 2 to 3 hours. Stir occasionally as the
ingredients settle.

2. Combine the shrimp and the marinade in a container.
Cover and refrigerate overnight.

The next day

3. Preheat a grill. Skewer the shrimp on bamboo or metal skewers and grill just until firm and browned on each side. Serve over rice or pasta, or on the skewers.

Southwestern Frittata

Joshua Grindle Inn
Mendocino, California
www.joshgrin.com

Last year, we held our first cooking class. It was more party than classroom! Eleven passionate foodies labored cooperatively to produce a spectacular Spanish-themed dinner. However, I burned the first entrée. After a slight regroup and a pitcher of sangría, the meal was deemed a success. I'm sure you'll have better luck with this longtime favorite.—CHRISTINE WAGNER, MANAGER

SERVES 16 TO 20

Vegetable oil or nonstick vegetable oil spray
14 to 16 corn tortillas, cut into 1-inch squares
27 ounces chopped canned green chilies
2 cans (2.25 ounces each) chopped black olives, drained

1¹/₂ cups marinated sliced or chopped red and
yellow bell peppers

1¹/₂ cups chopped tomato

1 cup chopped scallions

2 cups grated Cheddar cheese

2 cups grated Monterey Jack cheese

16 large eggs

1¹/₂ cups milk

1 teaspoon ground cumin

1 teaspoon onion salt

1 teaspoon garlic salt

1 teaspoon freshly ground black pepper

¹/₂ cup chopped fresh cilantro leaves

Fresh salsa, for serving

Sour cream, for serving

1. Lightly oil a 10 × 15-inch glass baking dish. In a large bowl, combine the tortillas, chilies, olives, peppers, tomato, and scallions. Add the cheeses and mix well. Spread evenly in the baking dish.

2. In a large mixing bowl, whisk together the eggs, milk, cumin, onion salt, garlic salt, black pepper, and cilantro. Mix well. Pour over the tortilla mixture in the glass baking dish. Cover and refrigerate overnight.

The next day

3. Preheat the oven to 350°F. Bake the frittata, uncovered, for 45 to 60 minutes, until lightly browned and bubbly. Serve with fresh salsa and sour cream on the side.

Salsa-Marinated Chicken with Spiced Orange Butter

Nantucket House of Chatham Bed & Breakfast
South Chatham, Massachusetts
www.chathaminn.com

When freezing chicken, open the package, rewrap the pieces into smaller portions, and place in zip-lock plastic bags. Thawing chicken in the microwave may make your chicken tough. Instead, try thawing it overnight in the refrigerator. The butter can be used for a number of foods (such as dressing steamed vegetables or topping grilled meats or grilled corn). The butter may be stored in the freezer for at least a month.

SERVES 6

FOR SPICED ORANGE BUTTER
1 cup (2 sticks) butter, at room temperature
6 tablespoons chipotle salsa, drained
$1/4$ teaspoon ground cinnamon
2 teaspoons finely grated orange rind
1 tablespoon chopped fresh cilantro leaves

FOR THE MARINADE
$1/2$ cup chipotle salsa
$1/2$ cup frozen orange juice concentrate, thawed
$1/4$ cup olive oil

¹/₄ cup soy sauce

2 tablespoons white wine vinegar

2 tablespoons honey

FOR THE CHICKEN

6 boneless, skinless chicken breast halves

2 large eggs

1 cup all-purpose flour

¹/₄ teaspoon salt

¹/₄ teaspoon freshly ground black pepper

¹/₈ teaspoon cayenne pepper

3 tablespoons olive oil, or as needed

Orange slices, for garnish

1. For the orange butter, place the ingredients in a food processor and process until smooth. Scrape the mixture out of the processor bowl onto a sheet of plastic wrap. Form into a cylinder about 1¹/₂ inches in diameter, wrap tightly, and place in the freezer.

2. For the marinade, place the ingredients in the same processor bowl and process until smooth. Reserve ¹/₄ cup of the marinade and empty the rest into a 1-gallon resealable plastic bag. Add the chicken to the marinade. Seal the bag and refrigerate overnight.

The next day

3. When ready to prepare the chicken, remove from the marinade and drain on paper towels. Discard the marinade from the bag. In a large shallow bowl, beat the eggs with a fork together with the reserved ¹/₄ cup marinade. In another wide, shallow bowl, combine the flour, salt, and black and cayenne peppers. Dip the chicken pieces in the egg mixture and then dredge in the flour mixture.

4. Heat the olive oil in a large, heavy skillet over medium-high heat. Cook the chicken until golden brown, turning once, about 6 minutes per side. To serve the chicken, remove the spiced orange butter from the freezer and slice into 12 equal pieces. Place 2 slices of the butter on each piece of hot chicken and garnish with the orange slices.

Potluck Casserole

Nantucket House of Chatham Bed & Breakfast
South Chatham, Massachusetts
www.chathaminn.com

You can't go wrong with this recipe. Have fun
emptying your refrigerator and creating new twists!

SERVES 8

1 cup uncooked rice
1 can (16 ounces) corn, drained
1 teaspoon salt
1 teaspoon freshly ground black pepper
2 cups canned tomato sauce
1 pound ground round or sirloin, browned
³/₄ cup chopped green pepper
¹/₂ cup chopped onion
6 ounces fresh spinach leaves, chopped
6 slices bacon

1. Spread the rice on the bottom of a 2¹/₂-quart casserole. Place the corn, salt, pepper, and 1 cup of tomato
sauce on top. Add the ground beef, green pepper, and
onion in layers. Top with the chopped spinach. Mix the remaining 1 cup of tomato sauce with ¹/₄ cup of water and
pour over the top. Top with the bacon slices. Cover and refrigerate overnight.

The next day

2. Preheat the oven to 350°F. Cover the casserole and
bake for 45 minutes. Uncover for the last 15 minutes to
brown on top.

Pork Loin Extraordinaire

Nantucket House of Chatham Bed & Breakfast
South Chatham, Massachusetts
www.chathaminn.com

The apples in this recipe should be soft. If they aren't, add a dash more wine to the mixture after the meat is removed; cover and place back in the oven until soft. Steamed asparagus is a good accompaniment.

SERVES 6

FOR THE SPICE RUB
1 tablespoon whole cumin seed
2 tablespoons brown sugar
1 teaspoon salt
1 teaspoon freshly ground black pepper
$1/4$ to $1/2$ teaspoon cayenne pepper

1 boneless pork loin (4 pounds), rinsed and dried
6 tablespoons olive oil
1 large Vidalia onion, peeled and sliced $1/4$ inch thick
2 or 3 thyme sprigs
3 large Granny Smith apples, peeled, cored, and sliced into $1/2$-inch-thick wedges
$1/4$ cup Riesling or other white wine

1. In a small nonstick skillet over medium-high heat, toast the cumin seed until aromatic. Allow to cool and grind finely.

2. Place in a zip-lock bag large enough to hold the pork loin and add the brown sugar, salt, and black and cayenne peppers; mix well. Add the pork loin to the bag and rub well with the spices. Seal the bag and refrigerate overnight.

The next day

3. Preheat the oven to 450°F. Place the olive oil in a flameproof, ovenproof casserole with a lid and add the pork loin and spices. Roll the pork to coat with the oil.

4. Place the casserole over medium-high heat and brown the meat on all sides. Transfer the pork to a plate. Return the pan to low heat, add the onion, and sauté until soft and translucent. Add the thyme sprigs and stir, covering the bottom of the pan with the onions. Layer the apple slices over the onion and cook briefly. Return the pork to the pan and pour the wine over all. Roast, uncovered, in the oven until a meat thermometer reads 150 to 155°F, about 40 minutes. Baste the roast with the wine periodically. If the bottom of the pan begins to dry out, add ½ cup of wine or water as needed. Remove the pork loin from the pan and allow to stand 10 to 15 minutes before carving. Spread the onion and apple mixture on a platter, with the sliced meat arranged over the top.

Marinated Vegetable Salad

Nantucket House of Chatham Bed & Breakfast
South Chatham, Massachusetts
www.chathaminn.com

Eating a diverse diet that includes five servings of vegetables per day can make your real age as much as four years younger.

SERVES 8

1 package (9 ounces) frozen halved artichoke hearts, thawed

1 package (10 ounces) frozen peas

$1/2$ cup vegetable oil

$1/4$ cup cider vinegar

$1/4$ teaspoon freshly ground black pepper

1 cup diagonally sliced baby carrots

1 cup diagonally sliced celery

$1/2$ cup fresh tiny broccoli florets

$1/2$ cup sliced red bell pepper

$1/2$ cup pimiento-stuffed green olives

$1/2$ cup pitted black olives

Salt

Romaine lettuce leaves, for serving

1. Cook the artichoke hearts and peas per package directions. Rinse with cold water and drain.

2. In a large bowl, combine the oil, vinegar, and black pepper; mix well. Add the drained artichoke hearts, peas, carrots, celery, broccoli, bell pepper, and olives. Mix well and season to taste with salt. Cover and refrigerate overnight.

The next day

3. Stir the salad and serve on romaine lettuce leaves.

Kitchen Garden Bread

Joshua Grindle Inn
Mendocino, California
www.joshgrin.com

This recipe has been a favorite of our guests for
years—twenty-five years, in fact! Kitchen Garden
Bread has an easy prep. It's fun to experiment with
substitutions.—CHRISTINE WAGNER, MANAGER

SERVES 20

Nonstick vegetable oil spray

1 round loaf (1 pound) sourdough bread

2 tablespoons vegetable oil

2 medium yellow onions, very thinly sliced

$^1/_2$ pound mushrooms, thinly sliced

1 tablespoon brown sugar

Salt

1 to 2 cups mixed fresh herbs and vegetables
(green onions, tiny broccoli florets, chives,
parsley, cauliflower, bell peppers)

8 ounces cream cheese

$^1/_2$ cup grated Cheddar cheese

$^1/_2$ to 1 pound hot pepper Jack cheese, grated

6 large eggs

1 cup milk

Chopped fresh herbs of your choice (optional)

1. Spray a baking sheet with nonstick spray. Slice the
bread in half so you have 2 rounds and scoop out most of
the soft center on each piece. Place the 2 halves on the baking sheet, cut-sides up, and set aside.

2. Place a large skillet over medium heat and add the oil. Sauté the onions and mushrooms for about 20 minutes, adding the brown sugar and a little salt about halfway through. Transfer to a plate and set aside.

3. Sauté the herb-vegetable mix until just tender, about 5 minutes. Transfer to a plate and set aside.

4. Cut the cream cheese into 1-inch cubes and distribute evenly over the bread. Top with the onion-mushroom mixture. Sprinkle with the Cheddar cheese. Top with half the herb-vegetable mix. Sprinkle on the pepper Jack cheese, then top with the remaining herb-vegetable mix.

5. In a mixing bowl, mix the eggs and milk together with any extra herbs you like and pour evenly over the bread. Cover and refrigerate overnight.

The next day

6. Preheat the oven to 375°F. Bake until the bread is thoroughly heated and the vegetable mixture is lightly browned on top, 35 to 40 minutes. Serve hot.

Vermont Cheddar Pie

Grunberg Haus Bed & Breakfast
Duxbury, Vermont
www.grunberghaus.com

A couple of years ago, we had a nice young woman
staying with us in one of our forest cabins. She
loved the area, but like many folks from the city,
she was concerned about wild animals, notably
bears. We had a somewhat lengthy discussion
about how wild animals behave, but we must have
left something out. The next day when we went to
her cabin for housekeeping, we found grocery sacks
with food left overnight on the deck to stay cool!
Later on, we explained to her the concept of "bait"
and that leaving food out will draw the animals she
wanted to avoid. That same morning at breakfast,
we overheard a couple complaining mildly to
another couple that the day before they had seen a
sign on the highway that said MOOSE 4 MILES. They
carefully watched the car's odometer and were sure
they had gone exactly four miles, but when they
arrived, there were no moose to be found!
They were disappointed in the lack of
accuracy in Vermont signs.
—LINDA & JEFF CONNOR, INNKEEPERS

SERVES 6

Vegetable oil or nonstick vegetable oil spray
2 cups frozen hash browns, thawed
1 medium onion, peeled and finely chopped
1 teaspoon seasoned pepper

¹/₃ cup grated Romano cheese
2 teaspoons garlic powder
¹/₃ cup frozen chopped spinach, thawed and drained
¹/₃ cup crumbled feta cheese
¹/₃ cup Vermont Cheddar cheese, grated
2 large eggs
¹/₂ cup milk
2 tablespoons dried parsley flakes
2 teaspoons paprika
Red salsa, for serving

1. Oil a 9-inch glass pie plate. In a medium bowl, combine the hash browns with all but ¹/₈ cup of the onion and press the mixture into the pie plate to form a crust. Sprinkle with the pepper, Romano cheese, and garlic powder, then dot with the spinach and feta cheese. Top evenly with the Cheddar cheese.

2. Whisk together the eggs and milk in a bowl and pour over the pie, working from the edge to the middle. Position the reserved chopped onion on top of the Cheddar cheese in the center of the pie. Sprinkle the parsley in a ring around the onion, then sprinkle the paprika around the parsley to make an outside ring. Cover and refrigerate overnight.

The next day
3. Preheat the oven to 350°F. Bake the pie, uncovered, until lightly browned, about 35 to 40 minutes. Allow to cool. Cut into 6 slices and serve with red salsa.

Spinach Lasagne

Alexander Bed & Breakfast
Gainesville, Texas
www.alexanderbnb.com

A fellow calligrapher made me a gift of a recipe
book with one recipe done in calligraphy in each
section. This is one of the recipes that I have used
often and am pleased to share. This cooking
method insures that the noodles will be done and
marries the flavors for a delicious vegetarian
lasagne. I have added Italian-flavored sausage at
times for those who do not want only spinach.
—PAMELA ALEXANDER, INNKEEPER

SERVES 8

Vegetable oil or nonstick vegetable oil spray

1 garlic clove, peeled and minced

1 package (10 ounces) frozen chopped spinach,
cooked and drained

1 jar (29 ounces) pasta sauce or your own homemade sauce

Italian seasoning to taste (basil, oregano)

6 to 8 uncooked lasagna noodles

15 ounces ricotta cheese

8 ounces sliced fresh mushrooms

1 pound grated mozzarella cheese

1/4 cup freshly grated Parmesan cheese

1. Preheat the oven to 350°F. Oil or spray an 8 × 8-inch
glass baking dish.

2. In a small bowl, mix the garlic with the spinach. Season the pasta sauce with the Italian seasoning to taste. Begin layering as follows: sauce, uncooked noodles (cut to fit the pan), ricotta, spinach, mushrooms, mozzarella. Repeat, ending with some sauce and mozzarella, topped with grated Parmesan cheese.

3. Bake, uncovered, until browned, about 30 minutes. Cool, cover, and refrigerate overnight.

The next day
4. Preheat the oven to 350°F. Bake the lasagne, covered, until thoroughly reheated, about 30 minutes.

Salmon Mexicana

Nantucket House of Chatham Bed & Breakfast
South Chatham, Massachusetts
www.chathaminn.com

I had cousins from France visiting Chatham and wanted to serve some type of seafood with a light touch of Mexican flair. Wanting to introduce them to the diversity of this area, I came up with this recipe. Sometimes I add $1/2$ cup of white wine as I simmer the vegetables.—MICHELLE KLEINKAUF

SERVES 8

2 tablespoons olive oil

1 large red onion, peeled and chopped

1 tablespoon minced garlic

12 ounces sliced fresh mushrooms

2 cans (15 ounces each) diced tomatoes with chilies and mild green peppers, drained

2 cans (15 ounces each) black beans, drained and rinsed

Salt and freshly ground black pepper

$2^{1}/_{2}$ pounds boneless salmon fillet, skin removed

$1/_{2}$ cup white wine (optional)

1. Place the olive oil in a skillet over medium heat. Add the onion and garlic and sauté until translucent. Add the mushrooms and sauté just until softened. Add the tomatoes and black beans and season to taste with salt and pepper.

178 · Sleep On It

2. Remove from the heat and allow to cool. Put into a tightly closed plastic container and refrigerate overnight.

The next day

3. Preheat the oven to 350°F. Place the salmon in a 9 × 12-inch glass baking dish and drizzle with the wine. Pour the sauce over the salmon and bake 30 minutes.

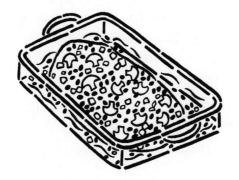

King Ranch Turkey

Jim Metzger
Chester, Virginia
Guest of the Nantucket House of Chatham Bed & Breakfast

This is a great way to serve leftover turkey after
Thanksgiving. Chop the turkey and sauté gently in
a tiny bit of olive oil with green onions and a little
ground cumin. Then construct the casserole per the
recipe and watch that turkey disappear!

SERVES 8 TO 10

FOR COOKING TURKEY

3 to 4 pounds uncooked turkey breast (or whole chicken)
1 onion, peeled and chopped
1 celery stalk, chopped
Salt and freshly ground black pepper

FOR ASSEMBLING CASSEROLE

1 celery stalk, chopped
1 can cream of mushroom soup
1 can mushroom soup
8 ounces grated Cheddar cheese
2 packages (8–10 count) corn tortillas (may not need all)
1 onion, peeled and chopped
1 large bell pepper, chopped
Chili powder
Garlic salt
1 can (12 ounces) tomatoes with chilies, drained,
briefly puréed in a blender

1. To cook the turkey, combine the turkey with the onion, celery, and salt and pepper to taste in a large pot. Boil until tender and thoroughly cooked, about 1 hour. Cut the turkey into bite-sized pieces and reserve all the stock.

2. To assemble the casserole, combine the celery, mushroom soups, and grated Cheddar in a large mixing bowl.

3. Just before putting the casserole together, dip the tortillas briefly in hot turkey stock until wilted. Start layering the casserole in a 9 × 12-inch baking dish in this order: tortillas dripping with stock, turkey, onion, bell pepper, chili powder, garlic salt to taste, and soup-cheese mixture. Repeat the layers, being sure the tortillas are oozing with stock. Cover the casserole with the puréed tomatoes and their juices. The juices in the casserole should be about half the depth of the pan. If not, add a little more turkey stock. Cover and refrigerate overnight.

The next day

4. Preheat the oven to 375°F. Bake the casserole, uncovered, for 30 minutes.

Karen's Chuck Steak

Nantucket House of Chatham Bed & Breakfast
South Chatham, Massachusetts
www.chathaminn.com

Kitchen tips : When shopping for beef, select it last
so that it is without refrigeration for the shortest
period of time. Work surfaces, dishes, and utensils
need to be washed thoroughly with hot soapy water
after use. Run your cutting board through the dish-
washer and use paper towels for cleanup.—C.G.

SERVES 3 TO 4

1 cup dry red wine
1 tablespoon Worcestershire sauce
1 tablespoon prepared white horseradish
2 tablespoons Dijon mustard
2 tablespoons ($1/4$ stick) butter, melted
1 tablespoon sugar
2 tablespoons minced onion
1 tablespoon parsley flakes
$1/2$ teaspoon salt
$1/2$ teaspoon oregano
1 teaspoon garlic salt
$1/4$ teaspoon Tabasco
$1^1/2$ pounds chuck steak

1. In a large rectangular glass dish, combine all the ingredients but the steak. Mix well and add the steak. Cover,
refrigerate, and marinate overnight.

The next day

2. Preheat a grill. Grill the steak 4 to 5 inches from the heat until cooked to taste, 20 to 25 minutes for rare. To serve, cut thinly against the grain of the meat.

Sweet Honey BBQ Shrimp

Nantucket House of Chatham Bed & Breakfast
South Chatham, Massachusetts
www.chathaminn.com

If you don't care for spicy shrimp, this recipe is your ticket for sweet shrimp on the barbie.

SERVES 10

1 onion, peeled and finely chopped

1 cup olive oil

$^1/_3$ cup honey

1 teaspoon sugar

1 teaspoon garlic powder

1 teaspoon cayenne pepper

$^1/_2$ teaspoon salt

$^1/_2$ teaspoon oregano

2 pounds large shrimp, shelled

1 pound bacon (optional)

Cooked rice or pasta, for serving (optional)

1. In a large bowl, combine the onion, oil, honey, sugar, garlic powder, cayenne pepper, salt, and oregano; mix well. Add the shrimp and mix again. Cover and refrigerate overnight.

The next day

2. Remove the marinated shrimp from the refrigerator an hour before grilling. Preheat a grill while skewering the shrimp on bamboo or metal skewers. If desired, wrap each skewer in a strip of bacon. Grill until the shrimp is opaque and the bacon is crisp. (Be careful of flames from the dripping marinade.) Serve over rice, pasta, or as is.

Homemade
Sausage Patties

55 East Bed & Breakfast
Annapolis, Maryland
www.55east.com

One day I was hurrying to make breakfast and I grabbed a plastic bag of yellow cheese out of the freezer and measured it into the quiche. The quiche cooked and I served it, noticing nothing unusual except that it didn't rise very high. When I

was making eggs the next morning, I grabbed for
the cheese again, only this time I wasn't as rushed.
As I started to pour it into the measuring cup, I
realized that it wasn't cheese at all. It was leftover
rice that I had cooked in orange juice for a meal the
past week!

These sausage patties can be crumbled and
used to add flavor to your favorite quiche recipe.
—MAT & TRICIA HERBAN, INNKEEPERS

SERVES 8

8 ounces ground turkey
8 ounces ground pork
$1/4$ teaspoon dried thyme
$1/4$ teaspoon ground allspice
$1/4$ teaspoon freshly ground black pepper
$1/2$ teaspoon salt
Canola oil, for frying

1. In a large mixing bowl, combine the ground turkey, ground pork, thyme, allspice, black pepper, and salt. Mix well and form into patties, using 2 tablespoons for each sausage. Wrap in plastic and refrigerate overnight.

The next day

2. Panfry the sausages in a small amount of canola oil.

Grandma's Meatloaf

Maggie and Ernie Doud
Glendale, California
Guests of the Nantucket House of Chatham Bed & Breakfast

This is a very simple but delicious third-generation meatloaf recipe. Use ground beef with 20 percent fat content. If you use less than that, it doesn't hold together well; more than that and it is too greasy.

SERVES 4 TO 6

1^1/$_2$ pounds ground beef
^{1}/$_4$ to ^{1}/$_2$ cup finely chopped onion
^{1}/$_2$ cup diced soft bread (about 1 slice)
^{1}/$_3$ cup chili sauce
1 large egg
Salt and freshly ground black pepper to taste

1. In a large mixing bowl, combine all the ingredients; mix well. Mound in a shallow glass baking dish or on a rimmed baking sheet and pat into a loaf. Cover and refrigerate overnight.

The next day

2. Preheat the oven to 350°F. Bake the meatloaf, uncovered, for 1 hour. Cut into slices to serve.

Soldier's Bread

The Strawberry Inn
New Market, Maryland

This recipe was handed down to me along with an
interesting story. Apparently the recipe got its name
because when soldiers went off on their tour of
duty, they would use coffee cans to cook out in the
fields. This bread is baked in coffee cans, thus the
name Soldier's Bread. This flavorful bread is
easy and fun.—JANE ROSSIG, INNKEEPER

MAKES THREE 1-POUND LOAVES

1¹/₂ cups raisins
2 cups hot water
2 tablespoons (¹/₄ stick) butter
2 teaspoons baking soda
Nonstick vegetable oil spray
4 cups all-purpose flour
2 cups sugar
2 large eggs, well beaten
1 teaspoon ground cinnamon
1 teaspoon pure vanilla extract
1 cup chopped walnuts, pecans, or other nuts

1. Mix the raisins, hot water, butter, and baking soda in a
bowl. Cover and let stand overnight.

The next day
2. Preheat the oven to 350°F. Coat the insides of three
1-pound coffee cans with nonstick spray.

3. Drain the raisins and place in a large mixing bowl. Add the flour, sugar, eggs, cinnamon, vanilla, and chopped nuts. Mix well. Distribute among the coffee cans, filling each can half full. Place the cans upright on a baking sheet and bake until risen, firm, and brown, about 1 hour.

4. Allow the bread to cool in the cans for at least 20 minutes. To remove the bread from a can, tap around the outside of the can, then turn the can over and gently shake until the bread slips out. Finish cooling the bread on a wire rack.

Gordon Family Stuffed Shells

Nantucket House of Chatham Bed & Breakfast
South Chatham, Massachusetts
www.chathaminn.com

You can't go wrong with these stuffed shells. Try using chicken or turkey instead of ground beef and use fresh spinach; add some drained small-curd cottage cheese or mix the ricotta with a little feta.

SERVES 6 TO 8

Nonstick vegetable oil spray
1 tablespoon cooking oil
1 pound ground beef
1 large egg

2 packages (10 ounces each) frozen chopped
spinach, thawed and drained

2 pounds ricotta cheese

2 cups mozzarella cheese

$^1/_3$ cup freshly grated Parmesan cheese

$^1/_2$ cup chopped onion

3 to 4 garlic cloves, peeled and minced

1 teaspoon salt

$^1/_4$ teaspoon oregano

$^1/_8$ teaspoon freshly ground black pepper

1 pound large pasta shells, cooked al dente (slightly
chewy), rinsed with cold water, and drained

Chopped parsley

2 jars (26 ounces each) spaghetti sauce

1. Oil a 9 × 13-inch glass baking dish and set aside. Place a large skillet over medium heat and add 1 tablespoon of oil. Add the ground beef and sauté until browned and crumbly. Place in a large mixing bowl and add the egg, spinach, ricotta, 1$^1/_2$ cups of mozzarella, 2 tablespoons of Parmesan, the onion, garlic, salt, oregano, and pepper; mix well.

2. Stuff the cooked pasta shells with the mixture and place in the glass baking dish. Sprinkle with the parsley and cover with the spaghetti sauce. Sprinkle the remaining Parmesan and mozzarella cheeses on top. Cover and refrigerate overnight.

The next day

3. Preheat the oven to 350°F. Bake the shells, uncovered, until lightly browned on top, about 45 minutes.

Eggplant : Parma Style

Nantucket House of Chatham Bed & Breakfast
South Chatham, Massachusetts
www.chathaminn.com

Eggplant facts : 1 pound eggplant = 3 to 4 cups
chopped eggplant, 1 medium eggplant = 1 pound.
Store your eggplant in a cool, dry place and use
within a day or two of purchase.

SERVES 4 TO 6

2 large eggplants (about 1^1/$_4$ pounds each)

Salt

1 cup light olive oil

6 slices prosciutto, sliced paper-thin

1 large red onion, peeled and sliced paper-thin

2 roasted red peppers (may be bottled)

^{1}/$_3$ cup grated Parmesan or Romano cheese, plus
another ^{1}/$_4$ cup for the topping

Freshly ground black pepper

1^1/$_2$ cups marinara sauce

3 tablespoons minced parsley

1. Slice the eggplants into ^{1}/$_2$-inch-thick rounds. Place
the rounds on baking sheets lined with paper towels.
Sprinkle with salt and let stand 2 hours to draw out the
bitter juices. Pat dry.

2. Place ^{1}/$_4$ cup olive oil in a large skillet over medium-
high heat. Fry the eggplant slices until brown on both
sides. Drain on paper towels.

3. In an 11 × 13-inch glass baking dish, make layers as follows: eggplant, prosciutto, onion, a few red pepper strips, a light dusting of cheese, sprinkling of ground pepper, about a third of the sauce. Repeat twice more, ending with the sauce. Cover and refrigerate overnight.

The next day

4. Preheat the oven to 350°F. Top the casserole with the cheese and parsley. Bake until browned, about 35 minutes. Cool slightly before serving.

Cream Biscuits

The Union Hotel
Benicia, California
www.unionhotelbenicia.com

Every meal is better with biscuits—biscuits and
gravy, sausage and biscuits, buttermilk biscuits,
fruit biscuits, and these Cream Biscuits.
The list goes on.

MAKES 20

4 cups all-purpose flour, plus additional as needed

2 tablespoons baking powder

1 teaspoon salt

$^1/_2$ cup (1 stick) good quality salted butter, plus
additional for the baking sheet

2 cups plus 1 tablespoon heavy cream

1. In a large bowl, stir together 4 cups of flour, the baking
powder, and salt. Using a pastry cutter or two knives, coarsely
cut in $^1/_2$ cup of butter. Add the cream gradually. Knead just
long enough to make a stiff dough. Do not overwork.

2. On a lightly floured surface, roll out the dough to a $^1/_2$-
inch thickness. Cut into squares of the desired size. Wrap
and refrigerate overnight.

The next day

3. Preheat the oven to 400°F. Butter a baking sheet or
cover with parchment paper. Place the biscuits onto the
baking sheet and bake until puffed and golden in color,
about 18 minutes. Serve immediately.

Chilies Con Queso

Old Monterey Inn
Monterey, California
www.oldmontereyinn.com

Chilies, popular in American Southwestern and Latin American cooking, lend an interesting spice to any meal. Seeds and the white ribs to which the seeds are attached hold its heat; for milder flavor, remove the seeds. To remove the chili seeds, you might want to wear rubber gloves and wash your hands with warm soapy water afterward.—C.G.

SERVES 6 TO 10

Nonstick vegetable oil spray

3 cans (7 ounces each) whole green chilies, drained and cut into chunks (seeds can remain)

3/4 pound provolone cheese, sliced or shredded

3/4 pound Cheddar cheese, sliced or shredded

4 ounces queso fresco cheese, crumbled
(can be found in the ethnic foods section)

1/2 cup milk

Dash of salt

3 large eggs

3/4 cup all-purpose flour

1. Spray a 9 × 13-inch glass baking dish with nonstick spray. (Alternatively, two smaller casseroles or individual dishes can be used instead.) Make layers in the dish as follows: one-fourth of the chilies, half the provolone, one-fourth of the chilies, all of the Cheddar, one-fourth of the chilies, half of the provolone, the remaining fourth of the chilies, and all the queso fresco.

2. In a small mixing bowl, blend together the milk, salt, and eggs. Mix until smooth. Gradually whisk in the flour until smooth. Slowly pour the mixture into the baking dish, gently pressing the cheese with a fork as you fill to prevent air pockets. Cover and refrigerate overnight.

The next day

3. Preheat the oven to 375°F. Bake the casserole, uncovered, until it puffs up and the top is turning brown, about 40 minutes. Serve immediately or cool and freeze for later use. (To cook the frozen casserole, leave in the refrigerator overnight to defrost, then bake as above or place the frozen casserole in the oven and cook for 60 minutes, until the center is hot and the casserole is browned.)

4. Cut into squares or rectangles to serve on a complementary colored dish accented with cilantro or parsley. Light corn bread and a mango, papaya, pineapple, and avocado salad will add some zesty flavors as well as a festive look.

Baked Swiss Corn

1884 Bridgeford House
Eureka Springs, Arizona
www.bridgefordhouse.com

This is good for brunch or as a side dish for dinner.

SERVES 4 TO 6

3 cups fresh cut corn or 2 packages
(9 ounces each) frozen corn

Salt

1 can (5^1/$_2$ ounces) evaporated milk

1 large egg, beaten

2 tablespoons chopped onion

Freshly ground black pepper

1 cup shredded Swiss cheese

^{1}/$_2$ cup soft bread crumbs

1 tablespoon butter, melted

1. In a saucepan, cook the corn in lightly salted water until tender. In a large bowl, combine the cooked corn, evaporated milk, egg, onion, ^{1}/$_4$ teaspoon salt, pepper to taste, and ^{3}/$_4$ cup of cheese. Mix and pour into a greased glass baking dish. Cover and refrigerate overnight.

The next day

2. Preheat the oven to 350°F. Toss the bread crumbs with the melted butter and remaining ^{1}/$_4$ cup of cheese. Sprinkle over the corn mixture and bake for 25 to 30 minutes.

Savory Spinach Crepes

Loghouse and Homestead on Spirit Lake
Vergas, Minnesota
www.loghousebb.com

Having many repeat guests, we needed some new
recipes. Our Savory Spinach Crepes with wine
sauce is now one of our most popular. Making these
crepes the night before gives the flavors time
to marry and meld. Once you make them, the
second time will be less time-consuming.
—SUZANNE TWETEN, INNKEEPER

SERVES 12

FOR THE CREPE BATTER (MAKES 24 CREPES)

2 cups all-purpose flour

1 cup whole milk

6 large eggs

$1/4$ cup ($1/2$ stick) butter, melted, plus additional as needed

1 teaspoon salt

3 teaspoons dried dill weed or 3 tablespoons
chopped parsley

FOR THE CREPE FILLING

$1 1/2$ pounds lean bacon, chopped

1 bunch scallions, white parts only, thinly sliced

12 ounces sliced mushrooms

3 boxes (10 ounces each) frozen spinach, thawed and
squeezed dry

$1/2$ teaspoon salt

$3/4$ teaspoon freshly ground black pepper

Small pinch of grated nutmeg

FOR THE WHITE SAUCE

6 tablespoons (³/₄ stick) butter

³/₄ cup flour

3 cups whole milk

1 teaspoon salt

1¹/₂ teaspoons freshly ground pepper

1 teaspoon lime juice, or more to taste

FOR THE WINE SAUCE

6 tablespoons (³/₄ stick) butter

¹/₄ cup finely chopped shallots

¹/₃ cup white wine

¹/₄ cup white wine vinegar

Parsley sprigs, for garnish

1. To make the crepe batter, combine 1¹/₄ cups water, the flour, milk, eggs, ¹/₄ cup melted butter, salt, and dill in a food processor. Process for 5 seconds, scrape down the sides, and blend for 20 seconds more. Pour into a bowl and chill at least an hour.

2. To make the crepes, preheat a crepe pan or small non-stick skillet over moderate heat and brush with melted butter. Pour in ¹/₄ cup batter and swirl to cover the bottom of the pan. Cook 1 minute, then turn and cook another minute. Turn onto wax paper and repeat the process, placing wax paper between each crepe, to make a total of 24 crepes. Cover the top crepe with wax paper and cover the stack loosely with plastic wrap. Refrigerate overnight.

3. To make the crepe filling, brown the bacon in a large skillet over medium heat, reserving several tablespoons of bacon fat for sautéing. Drain the bacon on paper towels.

4. Return the skillet to medium heat and add a tablespoon of bacon fat. Sauté the scallions and mushrooms until the mushrooms have softened and their liquid has almost evaporated. Transfer to a large heatproof bowl.

5. Add a tablespoon of bacon fat to the skillet and add the spinach. Sauté until no moisture remains. Stir in the salt, pepper, and nutmeg. Set aside while making the white sauce.

6. To make the white sauce, melt the butter in a saucepan over moderate heat. Add the flour and blend until smooth. Remove from the heat and add the milk all at once. Quickly whisk to blend, return to the heat, and cook until smooth, whisking constantly. Add the salt, pepper, and lime juice. Add to the reserved bowl of crepe filling and mix well. Cover and refrigerate overnight.

7. To make the wine sauce, place a small skillet over medium-low heat and melt the butter. Add the shallots and sauté until tender. Add ⅓ cup water, the wine, and vinegar and simmer until reduced by half. Transfer to a covered container and refrigerate overnight.

The next day

8. Preheat the oven to 300°F. Allow the crepes to come to room temperature. In a small saucepan, reheat the wine sauce and keep warm. Place the filling in its heatproof bowl, covered with foil, in the oven until thoroughly reheated.

9. To assemble the crepes, spread approximately ¼ cup filling on one quarter of a crepe. Fold the crepe over in half and again in a quarter. Place 2 crepes on each plate. Drizzle with wine sauce, garnish with a sprig of parsley, and serve.

Vidalia Onion Corn Casserole

Nantucket House of Chatham Bed & Breakfast
South Chatham, Massachusetts
www.chathaminn.com

Legend has it that Vidalia onions took root in
1931 in Toombs County, Georgia, when a farmer
named Coleman discovered the onions he had
planted weren't hot but sweet! Vidalia onions
have an international reputation as the
world's sweetest onion.

SERVES 6 TO 8

2 tablespoons (¼ stick) butter or margarine

3 medium Vidalia or other sweet onions, peeled and cut
into ¼-inch slices

½ pound sliced mushrooms

Vegetable oil or nonstick vegetable oil spray

2 cups shredded Cheddar cheese

1 can (12 ounces) creamed corn

1 can (5 ounces) evaporated milk

1 tablespoon soy sauce

6 slices French bread, cut ½ inch thick

⅓ cup chopped parsley

1. Place a large skillet over medium heat and melt the butter. Add the onions and mushrooms and sauté until tender. Place the mixture into a lightly oiled 2-quart glass casserole dish. Sprinkle with 1 cup of cheese.

2. In a mixing bowl, combine the creamed corn, evaporated milk, and soy sauce; pour over the cheese. Top with the French bread slices, then sprinkle evenly with the remaining cup of cheese and the chopped parsley. Cover and refrigerate overnight.

The next day

3. Preheat the oven to 375°F. Let the casserole stand at room temperature for 30 minutes. Bake the casserole, covered, for 30 minutes. Uncover and bake until thoroughly heated, 15 to 20 minutes more. Let stand 5 minutes before serving.

Baked Barbecued Beef Brisket

55 East Bed & Breakfast
Annapolis, Maryland
www.55east.com

This tastes like sloppy joes and is great served with mashed potatoes and corn bread. If you cook the meat ahead of time, the cold fat can be removed very easily from the top of the sauce. The meat cuts best when chilled.

SERVES 8

1 cup ketchup

$^1/_4$ cup minced onion or 1 tablespoon dried onion flakes

2 tablespoons cider vinegar

1 tablespoon prepared white horseradish

1 tablespoon prepared yellow (hot dog) mustard

1 teaspoon salt

$^1/_4$ teaspoon freshly ground black pepper

4 pounds boneless beef brisket

1. In a large bowl, combine all the marinade ingredients with 1 cup of water. Pour 1 cup of marinade into the bottom of a roasting pan that comfortably fits the meat. Place the brisket into the pan, fat-side up. Pour the remaining marinade over the brisket. Cover and refrigerate overnight.

The next day
2. Preheat the oven to 300°F. Cover the meat with a lid or foil and bake until tender, $3^1/_2$ to 4 hours. Remove the meat from the baking pan and keep warm on a platter. Skim the fat from the sauce. Slice the meat and serve the sauce separately.

Artichoke and Caper Bread Pudding

The Inn at Schoolhouse Creek
Little River, California
www.schoolhousecreek.com

During World War II, the property that is now
The Inn at Schoolhouse Creek was turned over to
the U.S. Coast Guard to house the shore patrol.
Today the inn continues to honor its history by
celebrating memories of times past, including
recipes from previous eras like this one.

SERVES 10

$1/2$ sourdough bread loaf, sliced

Nonstick vegetable oil spray

4 ounces cream cheese, cubed

1 cup grated Cheddar cheese

1 cup grated Monterey Jack cheese

1 cup sliced scallions

$1/4$ cup capers, rinsed and drained, or $1/4$ cup roasted red
peppers, drained

1 jar (6 ounces) marinated artichoke hearts, rinsed and
drained

5 large eggs

1 cup milk

$1/4$ teaspoon dry mustard

$1/4$ teaspoon dried thyme

Freshly ground black pepper to taste

$1/4$ teaspoon cayenne pepper

1. Slice the crust from the bread and cut the bread into 1-inch cubes. Spray a 9 × 13-inch glass baking dish with nonstick spray and place the bread cubes in the bottom. Dot with cream cheese. Layer the Cheddar, Monterey Jack, and scallions over the bread and top with the capers and artichokes.

2. In a separate bowl, beat the eggs well. Add the milk, dry mustard, thyme, black pepper, and cayenne pepper and mix well. Pour over the bread mixture, cover with foil, and press the bread down to soak up the egg mixture. Refrigerate overnight.

The next day

3. Preheat the oven to 375°F. Bake the pudding, covered, in the top third of the oven for 20 minutes. Remove the foil and bake until nicely browned and bubbly on top, about 20 more minutes. Let stand 10 minutes before cutting.

Crawfish or Shrimp Maquechoux

1870 Banana Courtyard French Quarter
New Orleans, Louisiana
www.bananacourtyard.com

Here in Louisiana we pronounce it *crawfish*, not
crayfish. Maquechoux (mock-SHOE) is a Cajun
word for a smothered dish made with fresh corn. If
crawfish is not available in your area, use all
shrimp. If white corn is not available, you may
substitute yellow corn, but it's not as traditional.
Substitute 1 pound frozen corn if fresh is not
available, then reduce the chicken stock from
2 cups to 1 cup. It's delicious!
—MARY & HUGH RAMSEY, INNKEEPERS

SERVES 8

2 packages (12 ounces each) frozen crawfish tails, thawed,
or 1 package crawfish and 1 pound medium shrimp,
peeled and deveined, or 2 pounds medium
shrimp, peeled and deveined

^{1}/$_2$ cup dry white wine

Juice of ^{1}/$_2$ lemon

Salt

8 to 10 ears of white corn on the cob, to yield
6 cups corn kernels

^{1}/$_3$ cup bacon drippings or olive oil

1 cup chopped green bell pepper

3 cups chopped onion

^{1}/$_4$ cup (^{1}/$_2$ stick) butter

2 tablespoons heavy cream, or more as needed

2 cups homemade or canned chicken stock
(do *not* use bouillon cubes)

3 large tomatoes, coarsely chopped, or 12 ounces
canned tomatoes, drained

1 teaspoon freshly ground black pepper

1/2 teaspoon Tabasco or other hot sauce

2 tablespoons finely chopped flat-leaf parsley

Corn bread, for serving (optional)

1. In a large bowl, marinate the crawfish or shrimp, wine, lemon juice, and 1/2 teaspoon salt.

2. Over a separate bowl, cut the corn kernels off the cobs; then scrape the cobs with a knife to get the liquid. Add the cob liquid to the bowl. (If using frozen corn, add 3 extra tablespoons heavy cream in place of the corncob liquid.)

3. In a large skillet, heat the bacon drippings or oil over medium heat. Sauté the bell pepper about 2 minutes, then add the onions and continue to sauté until the vegetables are softened but not browned.

4. Using a slotted spoon, transfer the vegetables to a bowl and return the skillet to medium heat. Add the corn, corn liquid, butter, cream, and chicken stock to the skillet and mix thoroughly. Sauté, uncovered, for about 10 minutes. Add the tomatoes and reserved onion and bell pepper and sauté over medium heat for 5 minutes.

5. Discard the crawfish marinade and add the crawfish or shrimp. Cook for 4 to 6 minutes, stirring frequently. If

the mixture seems too dry, add 2 to 3 tablespoons of water. Season with the black pepper and Tabasco. Adjust the
salt to taste. Place in a tightly covered bowl and refrigerate
overnight.

The next day
6. Reheat thoroughly, garnish with the parsley, and serve
in wide soup bowls. If desired, serve with corn bread.

Potato Florentine Egg Casserole

The Bedford Inn
Cape May, New Jersey
www.bedfordinn.com

One morning during breakfast, I felt an
unexplained tension at the table. Chatting
pleasantly with a number of couples, I could see
that two of the men were eyeing each other
strangely across the table. I began to bring them
into the general conversation and found that one
worked for a large corporation and the other for an
agency of the federal government. When this
information came out, they joyfully realized that for
many months in the course of their business day,
they spoke on the phone, working together on
a contract between the government and the
corporation. Each man was very familiar with the
other's voice but not his face. It turned out to be a

great weekend for them, enjoying Cape May and
getting to know each other face-to-face.

—ARCHIE & STEPHANIE KIRK, PROPRIETORS

SERVES 6

Vegetable oil or nonstick vegetable oil spray
1/2 box (2.5 ounces) dried au gratin potatoes
12 large eggs
3 tablespoons milk
1 teaspoon Worcestershire sauce
1 teaspoon sugar
1/4 teaspoon garlic powder
1/2 box (5 ounces) frozen chopped spinach, drained

1. Oil or spray a 9 × 9-inch glass baking dish. Place the
dried potatoes in a bowl of boiling water to soften. Set
aside the packet of cheese that comes with the potatoes.

2. While the potatoes soften, whisk together the eggs,
milk, Worcestershire sauce, sugar, garlic powder, and
spinach in a large bowl. Pour into the baking dish.

3. When the potatoes have softened (after about 15
minutes), drain and mix in half of the cheese packet. (Store
the remaining cheese and potatoes for another time.) Add
the potato mixture to the casserole. Cover and refrigerate
overnight.

The next day

4. Remove the casserole from the refrigerator and preheat the oven to 350°F. Bake, uncovered, until set, about
45 minutes. Cut into squares and serve hot.

Eggplant Mozzarella

Nantucket House of Chatham Bed & Breakfast
South Chatham, Massachusetts
www.chathaminn.com

If you don't want to fry the eggplant, spray a baking sheet with vegetable oil cooking spray and cover with eggplant slices. Bake at 350°F about 15 minutes on each side, until nicely brown. Transfer to a baking dish and layer as stated in the recipe.

SERVES 6

1 large eggplant

1 large egg, beaten

Seasoned bread crumbs

$1/4$ cup olive oil, or as needed

1 jar (23 ounces) spaghetti sauce
(homemade can be used as well)

1 to $1^1/2$ cups shredded fresh mozzarella cheese,
or thinly sliced

Grated Parmesan cheese, at room temperature

1. Peel the eggplant and cut into $1/4$-inch slices. Dip into the beaten egg and dredge in bread crumbs.

2. Place a large skillet over medium heat and add $1/4$ cup olive oil. Fry the eggplant over medium heat until lightly browned on each side, adding additional oil as needed. Drain on paper towels.

3. Place a layer of eggplant (may be slightly overlapping) in an ungreased 9 × 13-inch glass baking dish. Top with a layer of spaghetti sauce, another layer of eggplant, and the mozzarella and Parmesan cheeses. Cover and refrigerate overnight. (The dish may also be frozen at this point.)

The next day
4. Preheat the oven to 350°F. Bring the dish to room temperature. Bake until cheese is melted and bubbling, about 30 minutes.

Holiday Yeast Rolls

Nantucket House of Chatham Bed & Breakfast
South Chatham, Massachusetts
www.chathaminn.com

This recipe is a staple at all of our holiday dinners. The rolls make wonderful sandwiches for leftover meat. If you're planning to make a lot to use up leftovers, you may wish to omit the sea salt. The rolls with sea salt sprinkled on top do not keep well—the salt dissolves into the rolls.
—KATHERINE MIKKELSON

MAKES 24 ROLLS

4 cups all-purpose flour

$^1/_4$ cup sugar

2 packages dry yeast

$1^1/_2$ teaspoons salt

$^3/_4$ cup lukewarm milk (105 to 110°F)

$^1/_2$ cup lukewarm water (105 to 110°F)

$^1/_3$ cup butter, melted, plus additional for greasing the pans

2 large eggs

Sea salt

Poppy and/or sesame seeds

1. In a large bowl, combine 1¹/₂ cups flour, the sugar, yeast, and salt. In a small bowl, combine the milk, water, and ¹/₃ cup melted butter, using an instant-read thermometer to make sure the mixture is 105 to 110°F. Add to the dry ingredients. Using an electric mixer at medium speed, beat the mixture for 2 minutes.

2. Add 1 egg and ¹/₂ cup of flour and beat at high speed for 2 more minutes. Add the remaining 2 cups of flour and mix with a wooden spoon to make a soft dough. Place the dough in a bowl, grease the top with butter, cover tightly with plastic wrap, and refrigerate overnight.

The next day

3. Butter two baking sheets and set aside. Remove the bowl from the refrigerator and punch the dough down. Transfer the dough to a lightly floured surface and cut into 24 pieces of equal size. Shape into knots or another desired shape. Place the rolls about 2 inches apart on the baking sheets. Cover with a dish towel and let rise in a warm place until doubled in size, about 20 to 40 minutes.

4. Preheat the oven to 375°F. Beat the remaining egg in a small bowl, brush on top of the rolls, and sprinkle with sea salt, poppy seeds, sesame seeds, or any combination. Bake until golden brown, 15 to 20 minutes.

Monte Cristo Sandwiches

Nantucket House of Chatham Bed & Breakfast
South Chatham, Massachusetts
www.chathaminn.com

These sandwiches are perfect for an easy supper.
I like serving them with a side salad and apple-
sauce or other fruit.—SANDRA BRITTAIN

SERVES 8

Vegetable oil or nonstick vegetable oil spray
16 slices white bread, crusts trimmed
8 ham slices
8 turkey slices
8 Cheddar cheese slices
6 large eggs, beaten
3 cups milk
$1/2$ teaspoon onion salt
$1/2$ teaspoon dry mustard
1 box (6 ounces) cornflakes
$1/2$ cup (1 stick) butter, melted

1. Oil or spray a 9 × 12-inch glass baking dish. Arrange a single layer of 8 bread slices in the greased baking dish. Top each slice with a slice each of ham, turkey, and cheese. Cover with the 8 remaining slices of bread.

2. In a large bowl, combine the eggs, milk, onion salt, and dry mustard and pour over the sandwiches. Cover and re-frigerate overnight.

3. Preheat the oven to 350°F. In a large bowl, combine the crushed cornflakes with the melted butter; mix well. Top the sandwiches with the cornflake mixture. Bake until crisp and golden brown, about 1 hour.

Pearson's Pond Healthy Ham Quiche

Pearson's Pond Bed & Breakfast
Juneau, Alaska
www.pearsonspond.com

This prizewinning quiche recipe is especially good for people who are lactose intolerant or need to watch their cholesterol and fats. It is quick to fix and keeps well. If you use frozen premade crusts, before baking be sure to thaw them first and poke holes all over them to prevent air bubbles.
For those with a wheat allergy, try this cornmeal substitute: 3¼ cups cold water, 1 teaspoon salt, ½ teaspoon chili powder, 1¾ cups yellow or white cornmeal. Cook over medium heat until quite thick and stiff, about 8 minutes. Press the thick cornmeal mixture into the pie pans as a piecrust substitute.

MAKES 2 PIES/SERVES 8 TO 12

1 cup soft silken or firm tofu
1 cup rice milk or plain or vanilla soy milk
1 cup liquid egg product
¾ cup nonfat ricotta cheese

½ to 1 teaspoon hot curry powder

1 teaspoon granulated steak seasoning

¼ teaspoon garlic salt

½ teaspoon ground coriander

1 tablespoon chopped onion

1½ cups cubed or ground ham
(or substitute ¾ cup crumbled bacon or sausage)

About 3 ounces canned chopped mild chilies

1 medium red bell pepper
(or substitute a few sun-dried tomatoes)

1 medium yellow or green bell pepper

1 bag (10 ounces) nonfat shredded mozzarella cheese

4 ounces fresh mushrooms, sliced or cut in pieces

2 baked and cooled piecrusts

1. In the container of a blender, combine the tofu, rice milk, egg product, and ricotta. Add the curry powder, steak seasoning, garlic salt, coriander, and chopped onion and blend until smooth. Transfer to a covered container and refrigerate.

2. Combine the ham and peppers in a food processor and chop to the size of small peas. If they seem wet, drain in a colander for a few minutes.

3. Distribute the shredded cheese, mushrooms, and chopped ham and peppers in the piecrusts. Cover and refrigerate overnight.

The next day

4. Preheat the oven to 350°F. Pour the liquid mixture over the contents in the piecrusts. Bake until a knife inserted into the pie comes out clean, about 45 minutes. Let set at least 15 minutes, then cut into wedges and serve.

Chicken
Vegetable Terrine

The Peabody Hotel
Memphis, Tennessee
www.peabodymemphis.com

The Peabody's fountain is famous for its ducks.
Back in the 1930s, the general manager of the
Peabody and his friend returned from a hunting
trip. The men thought it would be funny to place
some of their live duck decoys (it was legal then for
hunters to use live decoys) in the beautiful Peabody
fountain. Three small English call ducks were
placed in the fountain, and the reaction was nothing
short of enthusiastic. Thus began a Peabody
tradition that has become internationally famous!
Today, the mallards are raised by a local farmer
and friend of the hotel. On retirement from their
Peabody duties, they are returned to the wild.
Though the Peabody is famous for our ducks,
we *never* serve duck on our menu!
—LINDA GREENWALD, EXECUTIVE ASSISTANT

SERVES 8

4 ounces green beans, trimmed
1 small zucchini, trimmed and thinly sliced lengthwise
1 medium carrot, trimmed, peeled, and thinly sliced
4 ounces asparagus, trimmed
4 ounces small fresh button mushrooms, stems cut off
4 cups tightly packed spinach, washed and stems removed
1 small onion, peeled and quartered

1^1/$_2$ pounds boneless, skinless chicken breasts, trimmed
of fat and cut into 1-inch pieces

1^1/$_4$ teaspoons salt

^{1}/$_4$ teaspoon freshly ground black pepper

2 large egg whites

1^1/$_2$ cups heavy cream

Butter, for greasing the pan

1. Using a steaming basket over boiling water and cooking one vegetable at a time, steam the green beans, zucchini, carrot, asparagus, and mushrooms just until tender.
Drain and reserve. Steam the spinach just until wilted, allow to cool, and squeeze out the excess water.

2. To make the chicken mousse, drop the onion through
the feed tube of a food processor with the metal blade in
place and the motor running. Process until finely chopped,
then add the chicken pieces and process until smooth.
Add the salt, pepper, egg whites, and spinach and process
for 30 seconds. With the motor running, slowly pour the
heavy cream through the feed tube until it is well blended.
Scrape down the workbowl and process 15 seconds more.
Cover and refrigerate overnight.

The next day

3. When ready to assemble the terrine, preheat the oven
to 350°F. Butter an 8^1/$_2$ × 4^1/$_2$ × 2^1/$_2$-inch loaf pan. Spoon
about 1 cup of the mousse into the pan and spread evenly
with a spatula. Use about half the carrot strips to make a
single layer, placing the strips about ^{1}/$_4$ inch in from the
sides of the pan. Cover the carrot layer with about 3 tablespoons of mousse. Top with the whole mushrooms, stem-

side down, and surround with the mousse, smoothing it across the top. Make a layer of asparagus, again covering with the mousse. Make a layer of zucchini and cover with the remaining mousse. Cover the terrine with foil, place in a shallow baking dish, pour boiling water halfway up the side of the pan, and bake in the center of the oven until a knife inserted in the center comes out clean, about 35 minutes. Remove to a wire rack and cool for 15 minutes. Pour off the juices, invert onto a cutting surface, and cut into 1/2-inch-thick slices with a serrated knife.

Artichoke and Roasted Pepper Soufflé

Joshua Grindle Inn
Mendocino, California
www.joshgrin.com

The simple life of an innkeeper is ever
changing and ongoing:

I is for incredible experiences with guests
N is for nice—most people you meet
N is for nifty new ideas to implement
K is for knowing what makes others feel
comfortable
E is for exciting moments
E is for exhausting days that pass you by
P is for pleasant smiles from your happy guests
E is for the earnest great life you lead
R is for the rewards of being the innkeeper who
makes a difference
—CHRISTINE WAGNER, MANAGER

SERVES 16 TO 20

Vegetable oil or nonstick vegetable oil spray

2 cans (13 ounces each) quartered artichoke hearts

1 can (4 ounces) sliced black olives

1 cup bottled chopped or sliced roasted red and
yellow bell peppers

2 cups shredded Cheddar cheese

2 cups shredded Monterey Jack cheese

12 large eggs

1 cup Bisquick

¹/₂ cup (1 stick) butter, melted
2 cups cottage cheese
1 teaspoon baking powder
Salt and freshly ground black pepper

1. Oil or spray a 10 × 15-inch baking pan and set aside. In a large mixing bowl, combine the artichoke hearts, olives, peppers, and Cheddar and Monterey Jack cheeses. Mix well and set aside.

2. In the bowl of a food processor, combine the eggs, Bisquick, melted butter, cottage cheese, and baking powder. Season to taste with salt and pepper. Process until smooth. Pour the egg mixture into the artichoke mixture and stir well. Pour into the baking pan, cover, and refrigerate overnight.

The next day

3. Preheat the oven to 400°F. Bake the soufflé, uncovered, until golden brown, about 30 minutes. Let stand for 5 minutes before cutting into squares. Serve hot.

Baked Cheese Grits

Howdy Pardner Bed & Breakfast
Cheyenne, Wyoming
www.howdypardner.net

This recipe is one of our guests' favorites. It can be divided in half and the second half—frozen, thawed, and cooked—will reheat well. The recipe was handed down to me from a friend who made a quadruple batch of it for her daughter's wedding dinner. It's a zesty alternative to potatoes. The Velveeta cheese works nicely in this recipe because it melts easily and has a mild flavor that marries nicely with the grits.—CALAMITY JAN, INNKEEPER

SERVES 8 TO 10

Vegetable oil or nonstick vegetable oil spray

1 teaspoon salt

³/₄ cup regular or quick-cooking grits
(do *not* use instant grits)

6 tablespoons (³/₄ stick) butter or margarine

8 ounces Velveeta cheese, cut into chunks

Dash of Tabasco, or to taste

2 large eggs, well beaten

Paprika

1. Oil or spray an 8 × 12-inch glass baking dish. Place 3 cups of water in a medium saucepan and bring to a boil. Add the salt and grits and cook until thickened, about 5 minutes. Remove from the heat and quickly beat in the butter, Velveeta, Tabasco, and eggs. Mix well until the

eggs are incorporated and the cheese has melted. Pour the mixture into the prepared pan. Cool, cover, and refrigerate overnight.

The next day

2. Preheat the oven to 350°F. Sprinkle the grits with paprika and bake until well heated and lightly browned on top, 40 to 45 minutes.

Seafood au Gratin

Breakfast on the Connecticut
Lyme, New Hampshire
www.breakfastonthect.com

A few years ago, we hosted a wedding and reception for a couple in the military. A week before the ceremony, it was determined that her father was too ill to attend. We came up with a video conference call where he could be a part of the ceremony through a TV. The bride was able to perform a special song she had written for her husband and her father. We were all so proud! This recipe was served also to rave reviews at the wedding. I always add more seafood, going heavy on the shrimp and using Alaskan King crab if available.—DONNA ANDERSEN, INNKEEPER

SERVES 6 TO 8

1 pound unpeeled shrimp

1 can (14 ounces) artichoke hearts,
drained and coarsely chopped

12 ounces lump crabmeat

$^1/_2$ to 1 pound scallops, lightly sautéed (not fully cooked)

$^1/_2$ pound lobster meat, or additional shrimp or scallops

2 cups (8 ounces) shredded sharp Cheddar cheese

$^1/_4$ cup ($^1/_2$ stick) plus 2 tablespoons butter

1 garlic clove, peeled and minced

2 tablespoons sliced scallions

8 ounces sliced fresh mushrooms

$^1/_4$ cup all-purpose flour

$^3/_4$ cup half-and-half

1 tablespoon chopped fresh dill or 1 teaspoon dried dill

$^1/_2$ teaspoon freshly ground black pepper

$^2/_3$ cup dry white wine

Vegetable oil or nonstick vegetable oil spray

FOR THE TOPPING (OPTIONAL)

$^1/_4$ cup bread crumbs

2 tablespoons ($^1/_4$ stick) butter, melted

1. Bring 4 cups of water to a boil in a large saucepan. Add the shrimp and cook until just opaque, about 3 minutes. Drain well and rinse with cold water. Peel and devein.

2. In a large bowl, combine the shrimp, artichoke hearts, crabmeat, scallops, lobster, and 1 cup shredded cheese; set the mixture aside. Place a large skillet over medium heat and melt 2 tablespoons of the butter. Add the garlic, scallions, and mushrooms and sauté until tender; drain. Stir the sautéed vegetables into the seafood mixture.

3. Melt the remaining butter in a large, heavy pan over low heat. Add the flour and cook 1 minute, stirring constantly, until smooth. Gradually add the half-and-half; cook over medium heat, stirring constantly, until thickened and bubbly. Remove from the heat and add the dill, pepper, and remaining 1 cup of shredded cheese, stirring until the cheese melts. (Do not be concerned if it seems very thick.) Gradually stir in the wine. Cook over medium heat until warm and thickened.

4. Oil or spray a 9 × 9-inch glass baking dish. Add the sauce to the seafood mixture and mix well. Spoon into the baking dish, cover, and refrigerate overnight.

The next day
5. Preheat the oven to 350°F. Remove the baking dish from the refrigerator and let stand at room temperature for 30 minutes. If desired, make a crumb topping by mixing the bread crumbs with the melted butter in a small bowl. Bake, uncovered, until lightly browned, about 45 minutes.

Baked Spinach and Cheese Grits

First Colony Inn
Nags Head, North Carolina
www.firstcolonyinn.com

We've found this recipe to be a staple of Southern church suppers. It can be cooked in 4-ounce soufflé dishes for individual servings to use as needed. If frozen or refrigerated, remove the dishes from the refrigerator. Let sit 30 to 40 minutes at room temperature. Preheat the oven to 350°F. Bake 10 to 15 minutes, until heated through, or microwave on high about 4 to 5 minutes.

—CAMILLE LAWRENCE, PROPRIETOR

SERVES 24 TO 30

2 bags (1 pound each) frozen chopped spinach

2 cups chopped parsley, stems removed

Nonstick vegetable oil spray

6 tablespoons grated Parmesan cheese

3 cups quick-cooking grits

$^1/_4$ cup ($^1/_2$ stick) margarine

$2^1/_2$ cups shredded Mexican-blend cheese

1 tablespoon minced garlic

1 tablespoon freshly ground black pepper

6 large eggs, lightly beaten

1 jar (4 ounces) sliced pimientos

1. Put the spinach into a colander to thaw. Blanch the parsley in 3 cups boiling water for 2 minutes. Pour the parsley and water into the colander with the spinach and drain. Squeeze out the water and chop the greens lightly if needed. Spray a 9 × 13-inch pan with nonstick spray and sprinkle the bottom with 3 tablespoons of Parmesan cheese.

2. Fill a large saucepan with 8 cups of water and bring to a boil over high heat. Whisk the grits into the boiling water and simmer, stirring, 5 minutes. Scrape into a large mixing bowl. Stir in the margarine and Mexican cheese. Stir the garlic and pepper into the beaten eggs and mix well into the grits mixture. Pour into the glass baking dish and sprinkle with the remaining 3 tablespoons of Parmesan cheese. Cover and refrigerate overnight.

The next day

3. Preheat the oven to 350°F. Garnish the grits with a ring of diced pimientos. Bake just until a knife inserted in the center comes out clean, about 20 minutes; do not overcook. Serve immediately or cover and refrigerate up to 2 days.

Chicken Logan
au Peche

Logan Inn
New Hope, Pennsylvania
www.loganinn.com

The Logan Inn (built in 1722), located close to the Delaware River, became an inn in 1727 and is one of the five longest-running inns in the United States. It is not documented that George Washington stayed here, but because the inn was open year-round, many soldiers did stay. Today our guests sometimes go home with more than just their vacation photos. They have written that they have found "orbs" of ghosts in their photos. We have yet to have "Emily," our most well-known ghost, join us for dinner, but you just never know.—CARL & PAM ASPLUNDH, PROPRIETORS

SERVES 4

4 large boneless, skinless chicken breast halves

Salt

White pepper

2 tablespoons ($1/4$ stick) butter

1 tablespoon brown sugar

$1/4$ teaspoon grated fresh ginger
or $1/2$ teaspoon minced candied ginger

1 ripe peach, peeled, pitted, and sliced

1 tablespoon Major Grey's chutney (optional)

About $1/2$ cup all-purpose flour

3 large eggs, beaten

³/₄ cup dry bread crumbs
Vegetable oil, for frying

1. Flatten the chicken breasts between sheets of wax paper as thin as possible without tearing. Season to taste with salt and pepper.

2. In a small saucepan, melt the butter. Add the sugar and ginger and stir until the sugar is dissolved. Add the peach slices and simmer for 1 minute. Cool and stir in the chutney, if using. Place the peach slices and a bit of their juice in each flattened breast. Fold by lifting one long end of the breast over the peaches, then tucking in the sides, then folding the other long end over all. Cover and refrigerate overnight.

The next day
3. Dust each folded chicken breast with flour, then dip in the beaten egg and roll in the bread crumbs. Refrigerate until ready to cook. Place a large skillet over medium heat and add enough oil to come about 1¹/₂ inches up the side of the pan.

(Alternatively, a deep-fryer may be used, heated to 350°F.) Heat the oil until shimmering and fry the folded chicken breasts until golden brown, about 10 minutes. Drain and serve.

Fillet of Sole
Stuffed with Shrimp

Trail's End—A Country Inn
Wilmington, Vermont
www.trailsendvt.com

Give a man a fish, feed him for a day. Teach
a man to fish, feed him for life.
—OLD NEW ENGLAND PROVERB

SERVES 6 TO 8

FOR THE STUFFED SOLE
$1/4$ cup ($1/2$ stick) butter
3 garlic cloves, peeled and minced
3 small onions, peeled and finely chopped
1 green bell pepper, cored and finely chopped
36 medium shrimp, peeled, cooked, and chopped
1 cup bread cubes
3 tablespoons chopped parsley
$3/4$ teaspoon salt
$1/4$ teaspoon freshly ground black pepper
6 pounds fillet of sole
2 cups (4 sticks) butter

FOR THE HOLLANDAISE SAUCE
3 egg yolks
1 tablespoon lemon juice
Cayenne pepper
$1/2$ cup (1 stick) butter
Paprika

1. For the stuffed sole, place a large sauté pan over medium heat and melt the butter. Add the garlic and onions and sauté until tender, about 3 minutes. Add the green peppers and cook for 1 minute. Add the shrimp, bread cubes, and parsley. Season to taste with the salt and pepper. Sauté for 5 minutes, then remove from the heat.

2. Place 2 tablespoons of the shrimp mixture on each fillet. Roll up and secure with a toothpick. Wrap and refrigerate overnight.

The next day

3. Preheat the oven to 350°F. Melt 2 cups of butter in a large baking dish. Roll each fillet in butter and arrange in the same dish. Bake until browned, about 30 minutes. If desired, while the fillets are baking, prepare the hollandaise sauce.

4. For the hollandaise sauce, combine the egg yolks and lemon juice in a blender. Season to taste with cayenne pepper. In a saucepan, melt the butter. Blend the yolk mixture on high for a few seconds, then slowly add the butter through the opening in the top of the blender container.

5. To serve, pour the hollandaise over each fillet and/or sprinkle with paprika.

Dessert

The best for last? Try our Coffeecake
Cookies (page 260), fresh from the heart of
Pennsylvania Dutch Country. The Apfelkuchen
(German Apple Cake) (page 242) takes a little
preparation but is well worth the effort. Or, if
you're in the mood for a custard, the Almond
Featherbeds (page 251) are amazing.

Vietnamese Bread Pudding

Brewery Gulch Inn
Mendocino, California
www.brewerygulchinn.com

This bread pudding is a traditional dish of
Vietnam and marries the flavors of
banana and coconut.

SERVES 12 TO 14

Vegetable oil or nonstick vegetable oil spray

1^1/$_2$ cups coconut milk (canned is fine)

2 cups half-and-half, milk, or cream

1 cup sugar

5 large eggs

4 ripe bananas, peeled and mashed

2 teaspoons pure vanilla extract

1 teaspoon ground cinnamon

1 loaf day-old French bread, crusts removed (stale
croissants are good for this, too), cut into 1-inch cubes

Lightly sweetened whipped cream, for serving (optional)

Sliced mangoes and pineapple, for serving (optional)

1. Oil or spray a 9 × 13-inch glass baking pan, and set
aside. In a large bowl, beat together all of the ingredients
except for the bread. Add the bread cubes and fold together. Spread evenly in the pan and cover with plastic
wrap. Refrigerate overnight.

The next day

2. Preheat the oven to 350°F. Bring a kettle of water to a boil. Place the pan of bread pudding inside a roasting pan or other pan large enough to hold it. Pour boiling water in the outside pan to come about halfway up the side of the pudding pan.

3. Place in the oven and bake until browned and firm to the touch, about 1 hour. Let stand for 30 minutes before serving. If desired, serve with lightly sweetened whipped cream and fresh fruit, such as sliced mangoes and pineapple.

Apple, Blue Cheese, and Bacon Cheesecake

Carlisle House
Carlisle, Pennsylvania
www.thecarlislehouse.com

This recipe was adapted from a recipe printed in the *Washington Post* several years ago. The cheesecake is very popular as well as easy to make. However, not all ovens are created equal. When cooking at low temperatures, check the heat with an oven thermometer to ensure it's not too high. If in doubt, set the oven to 185°F.

SERVES 16 TO 20

Nonstick vegetable oil spray

$1/2$ cup freshly grated Parmesan cheese

8 ounces bacon, sliced

1 onion, peeled and chopped

2 apples, peeled, cored, and diced into medium cubes

2 garlic cloves, peeled and minced

Salt and freshly ground black pepper

2 pounds cream cheese, at room temperature

3 tablespoons white wine vinegar

$1/4$ cup whiskey

12 ounces crumbled blue cheese

5 large eggs

Thinly sliced fresh apples, for garnish
(if desired, dress with lemon juice to prevent discoloration)

1. Before going to bed, preheat the oven to 200°F. Spray the inside of a 9-inch springform pan with nonstick spray and dust the bottom and sides with 3 tablespoons of the Parmesan cheese. Set aside.

2. In a skillet, cook the bacon until crisp; remove, drain, crumble, and reserve. Discard all but 2 tablespoons of the bacon fat. Add the onion to the fat and cook over medium heat until softened, about 2 minutes. Add the cubed apples and continue cooking until the onion is very tender and the apples have lost their raw look, 2 to 3 minutes. Remove from the heat and add the garlic and salt and pepper to taste. Set aside.

3. In a large bowl, beat the cream cheese until soft. Mix in the vinegar, whiskey, blue cheese, remaining Parmesan cheese, and eggs. Add salt and pepper to taste, the reserved bacon, and the reserved apple mixture. Mix well, pour into the prepared pan, and place in the center of the oven. Go to bed. If possible, plan to check the cake after 7 or no longer than 8 hours in the oven.

The next day

4. The cake will appear set. The top will have barely colored and the surface will be smooth. Remove to a rack and cool in the pan for an hour until the pan is cool enough to handle.

5. Cover with a sheet of plastic wrap or wax paper and an inverted plate. Holding the plate tight to the pan, invert both. Remove the pan and refrigerate the cake upside down for at least 1 hour. The inverted cake can stay refrigerated all day.

6. Invert a serving plate over the cheesecake and invert the whole thing. Remove the top plate and the paper. Cover and refrigerate. Serve as is or garnish with freshly sliced apples.

Banana Chantilly

The Lodge on the Desert
Tucson, Arizona
www.lodgeonthedesert.com

Our guest was going to propose and we wanted to provide a perfect romantic setting with a unique dessert. We thought Bananas Foster would be just the thing, that is, until I almost burnt down the kitchen making the flambé. On to Plan B, Banana Chantilly. Thanks to The Lodge on the Desert and their Banana Chantilly, our efforts were a success. She said "Yes!" and we all lived happily ever after!—C.G.

SERVES 6 TO 8

3 large egg whites

³/₄ cup sugar

¹/₂ teaspoon pure vanilla extract

¹/₄ teaspoon vinegar

1 cup mashed bananas

¹/₄ teaspoon salt

1¹/₂ tablespoons lemon juice

¹/₂ cup whipping cream

Mint leaves and red cherries, for garnish

1. Preheat the oven to 275°F. Using an electric mixer in a mixing bowl, beat the egg whites until nearly stiff. Gradually add the sugar, beating constantly. Add the vanilla and vinegar and beat until stiff and well blended. Divide the mixture in half. Spread each half over a 3 × 9-inch area of a baking sheet. Bake until delicately browned, 40 to 50 minutes. Remove from the oven and allow to cool.

2. Combine the mashed bananas with salt and lemon juice in a bowl. Whisk the heavy cream into the banana mixture. Place one baked meringue on a baking sheet and cover with the filling. Top with the second meringue. Cover with plastic wrap and freeze overnight.

The next day

3. To serve, slice into 6 to 8 portions and top each with mint leaves and a red cherry. Serve immediately.

Chocolate-Covered Peanut Butter Balls

Nantucket House of Chatham Bed & Breakfast
South Chatham, Massachusetts
www.chathaminn.com

Everyone who has tasted these peanut butter
balls has requested the recipe. Wrap them
individually in plastic ; tie with a pretty
ribbon—good for Easter baskets !

MAKES 24 CONFECTIONS

1 pound confectioners' sugar
2 cups chunky peanut butter
$^1/_2$ cup (1 stick) butter, softened
$3^1/_2$ cups Rice Krispies
1 package (12 ounces) chocolate chips, melted

1. In a large bowl, combine the confectioners' sugar, peanut butter, butter, and Rice Krispies. Mix with your hands and roll into walnut-size balls. Refrigerate overnight.

The next day

2. Dip the balls into melted chocolate and put on wax paper to set.

Mexican Bread Pudding

River Run B&B Inn
Kerrville, Texas
www.riverrunbb.com

Apricots, known as the "romantic roses" of fruits, come from a tree of the rose family. The ancient Chinese considered this delicate fruit to be a symbol of a sensual nature. In addition, the apricot is reputed to be the prime fruit in the Garden of Eden and quite possibly the "apple" with which Eve tempted Adam. What better fruit to be included in a Mexican Bread Pudding, called a Capirotada in its home country.

SERVES 10

FOR THE BREAD PUDDING

$^1/_2$ cup dried apricots, chopped

$^1/_2$ cup (1 stick) butter or margarine, melted

1 loaf French bread, cut into 2-inch cubes

$^1/_2$ cup sugar

4 large eggs

2 cups milk

2 teaspoons vanilla

1 teaspoon cinnamon

$^1/_2$ teaspoon salt

FOR THE CAJETA SAUCE

1 cup (packed) brown sugar

$^1/_2$ cup chopped pecans

$^1/_2$ cup coconut flakes

$^1/_4$ cup apricot nectar

3 tablespoons apricot brandy

1. Preheat the oven to 375°F. Place the chopped dried apricots in a microwaveable glass bowl; cover with water and microwave for 2 minutes. Set aside.

2. Pour half the melted butter into a 9 × 12-inch glass baking pan. Spread the bread cubes over the bottom of the pan. Place in the oven for 15 minutes. Meanwhile, in a large bowl, cream the sugar into the remaining $^1/_4$ cup butter. Beat in the eggs, then the milk, vanilla, cinnamon, and salt.

3. Remove the pan from the oven. Drain the apricots and sprinkle over the bread cubes. Then evenly pour the egg-milk mixture into the pan. Cover and refrigerate overnight.

The next day

4. Preheat the oven to 375°F. Bring a kettle of water to a boil. Remove the pan from the refrigerator and let stand 30 minutes at room temperature. Place the glass pan inside a roasting pan or baking pan large enough to hold it. Add enough boiling water to come about $^1/_2$ inch up the side of the glass pan. Loosely cover the glass pan with foil. Bake for 20 minutes. Remove foil covering and bake until a toothpick inserted into the center comes out dry, 15 to 20 more minutes. Remove from the oven to cool for 20 minutes before serving. If desired, serve with Cajeta sauce.

5. For the Cajeta sauce, in a small saucepan, combine the brown sugar, pecans, coconut flakes, apricot nectar, and apricot brandy. Stir until the sugar is dissolved and the mixture is slightly thickened. Serve warm, drizzled over the pudding.

Almond Pear Clafouti

Good Medicine Lodge
Whitefish, Montana
www.goodmedicinelodge.com

This French dessert is usually made by topping
a layer of fresh fruit with batter. Although it
is often served with cream, it can also
have a pudding topping.

SERVES 6 TO 8

Butter, for greasing baking dish
4 firm-ripe pears, peeled, cored, and sliced
2 tablespoons fresh lemon juice
3/4 cup sliced blanched almonds
3/4 cup milk
8 tablespoons (1 stick) unsalted butter, melted and cooled
3 large eggs, beaten lightly
1/2 teaspoon pure vanilla extract
1/2 teaspoon pure almond extract
3/4 cup self-rising cake flour
1/2 cup plus 2 tablespoons sugar
Pinch of salt

1. Butter a 10 × 2-inch round (1-quart capacity) glass baking dish. In the dish, toss the pears gently with the lemon juice and spread them out evenly. In a blender, grind fine $1/2$ cup of almonds; add the milk, 6 tablespoons of melted butter, the eggs, and vanilla and almond extracts, and blend the mixture until smooth. In a bowl, whisk together the flour, $1/2$ cup of sugar, and salt and stir in the milk mixture, stirring until the batter is combined well. Pour the batter over the pears, cover, and refrigerate overnight.

The next day

2. Preheat the oven to 400°F. Drizzle the clafouti with the remaining 2 tablespoons melted butter and sprinkle it with the remaining 2 tablespoons sugar and $1/4$ cup almonds. Bake the clafouti in the middle of the oven for 40 minutes, or until golden brown. Let it cool on a rack for 15 minutes. Serve warm.

Apfelkuchen
(German Apple Cake)

The Chalet Inn
Dillsboro, North Carolina
www.ChaletInn.com

This is great for breakfast, brunch, or as a special birthday cake. Try making decorative strips out of the remaining dough to cover the filling. If the dough tears, it's easy to repair!

SERVES 6 TO 8

1^1/$_3$ cups (11 ounces) self-rising flour

1 cup sugar

^{2}/$_3$ cup butter

2 egg yolks

Pinch of salt

1 pound cooking apples, peeled, cored, and sliced
(or use drained canned apple rings)

Juice of 1 lemon

Pinch of ground cinnamon

^{1}/$_4$ cup raisins

^{1}/$_4$ cup ground hazelnuts

^{1}/$_4$ cup ground almonds

2 tablespoons apricot jam

^{1}/$_4$ cup homemade or canned vanilla icing

2 tablespoons kirsch (cherry liqueur)

1. Sift the flour into a bowl. Stir in ^{2}/$_3$ cup of sugar and knead in the butter. Add the egg yolks and salt and mix to a smooth dough. Chill for 20 minutes. Roll out half the dough to cover the bottom of a $9^1/_2 \times 3$-inch-high spring-form pan; return the remaining half to the refrigerator until needed.

2. Preheat the oven to 400°F. Bake the pan with the dough for 15 minutes. Remove the pan from the oven, but do not turn off the oven.

3. In a large mixing bowl, combine the apples with the remaining $^1/_3$ cup of sugar. Add the lemon juice, cinnamon, raisins, hazelnuts, and almonds. Moisten with a little water to blend. Spoon evenly onto the baked pastry shell in the springform pan.

4. Roll out the remaining dough and, using a spatula to lift it, carefully cover the filling. Bake for 30 minutes. Cool in the pan overnight.

The next day

5. An hour before serving, remove the sides from the springform pan and allow the cake to reach room temperature. Shortly before serving, warm the jam and spread over the cake. Combine the icing and kirsch in a small bowl and drizzle over the jam.

Black Raspberry Crepes

The Artist's Inn and Gallery
Terre Hill, Pennsylvania
www.artistinn.com

You just never know where the conversation
will lead at breakfast. Guests were talking one
morning about how they met. One couple met in
high school, another couple met at work. The third
couple was an older couple and they just grinned at
each other until she said, "I met my husband at his
wife's funeral!" After a brief pause, everyone
laughed and continued with their stories.

Any crepe can be used in this recipe. I like to
make my crepes the day before, laying wax paper
between each crepe. Wrap them in plastic and
store in the fridge overnight. They also freeze well.
Wrap in foil and reheat in the oven just before
serving. The filling takes just a few
minutes the next morning.
—JAN & BRUCE GARRABRANDT, INNKEEPERS

SERVES 7 TO 8

FOR THE CREPES (MAKES ABOUT 16)
3 tablespoons butter
1 cup all-purpose flour
$^1/_4$ cup confectioners' sugar
1 cup milk
2 large eggs
1 teaspoon pure almond extract
$^1/_4$ teaspoon salt

3 cups black raspberries
3 tablespoons butter
$^1/_4$ cup sugar
$^1/_4$ teaspoon finely grated lemon zest
1 teaspoon cornstarch

FOR ASSEMBLY
Butter, for greasing the baking dish
Lightly sweetened whipped cream, for serving

1. For the crepes, place a small skillet over medium-low heat and add the butter. When the butter has melted, pour it into a blender container and add the flour, confectioners' sugar, milk, eggs, almond extract, and salt. Mix until thoroughly blended.

2. Return the small skillet to medium heat. When the pan is hot, pour in about $^1/_4$ cup of the batter and swirl the pan to spread a thin layer over the bottom. Cook until lightly browned, flip, and brown the other side. Place the crepes on a plate with wax paper layered between them to keep them from sticking. The crepes can now be wrapped in plastic and refrigerated overnight.

3. For the filling, combine the raspberries, butter, sugar, 2 tablespoons of water, and the lemon zest in a small saucepan. Cook over medium heat until the sugar is melted and the liquid is smooth. Strain and reserve the berries. Add the cornstarch to the sugar mixture and boil, stirring constantly, until thick. Return the raspberries to the mixture and stir until just combined. The mixture may be cooled and refrigerated overnight.

The next day

4. Preheat the oven to 350°F. Butter a 9 × 13-inch glass baking dish. Spoon 2 teaspoons of filling into a crepe. Roll up and place in the baking dish. Repeat until all the filling is used. Cover loosely with foil and heat in the oven until warm, about 20 minutes. Serve topped with lightly sweetened whipped cream.

Cointreau Apples

Limestone Inn
Strasburg, Pennsylvania
www.limestoneinn.com

One morning, with a full house, we were making
our Cointreau Apples. We had removed the pan
from the refrigerator but had not yet begun to bake
them. We were in the other room, chatting with
some early risers, and when we came back into the
kitchen, Alex, our 100-pound yellow Lab, was lying
on the floor, "resting." Thinking this was a little
odd, we went to the counter to put the pan into the
oven and, lo and behold, we had a completely clean
pan! Not a drop of anything was left and the pan
was generally undisturbed right where it was on
the counter. The mystery of Alex's nap was
solved—she had finished off the entire pan of
Cointreau Apples in just a few seconds and was
sleeping it off. Needless to say, she is now
banished to our office during cooking hours. We
found that if we turn on the range hood fan,
the noise keeps her out of the kitchen.
—RICK & DENISE WALLER, INNKEEPERS

SERVES 6 TO 8

$^1/_2$ cup freshly squeezed lemon juice
$^1/_2$ cup freshly squeezed orange juice
6 Granny Smith or other tart baking apples
1 cup dried cranberries or raisins
1 ounce Cointreau liqueur
$1^1/_2$ cups (3 sticks) butter

$^1/_2$ cup brown sugar, or to taste

Ground cinnamon

Whipped cream or crème fraîche, for serving

1. Mix the lemon and orange juices in a small bowl and pour into a 9 × 13-inch glass baking dish. Peel and core the apples and slice into eighths.

2. Gently toss the apple slices in the juice solution, making sure to coat well to prevent browning. Top the apple slices with the dried cranberries and drizzle with the Cointreau.

3. Slice the butter into small slices and scatter on top of the apples. Sprinkle with the brown sugar and add cinnamon to taste. Cover tightly with plastic wrap and refrigerate overnight.

The next day

4. Preheat the oven to 350°F. Bake the apples, uncovered, for about 20 minutes, basting frequently to keep them from drying and burning. The apples should be slightly soft but not mushy.

5. To serve, spoon the apples while hot into bowls, top with fresh whipped cream or crème fraîche, and then spoon a little of the juice and cranberries from the pan over the top of the whipped cream. Serve immediately.

Baked and Puckered Englishman

The Inn at Harbour Ridge
Osage Beach, Missouri
www.harbourridgeinn.com

Since pineapple is the symbol of hospitality, as an innkeeper/owner I try to find fun recipes using it as an ingredient. However, some of my younger guests aren't very appreciative of pineapple, so I've changed an ingredient from the original recipe and made up a silly name to go along with this variation of baked pineapple. Instead of white bread cubes, I use English muffins, hence the name Baked and Puckered Englishman! We always laugh and tell our guests that there's nothing stuffy about our inn. Guests can't wait to find out what it is.
—SUE WESTENHAVER, INNKEEPER

SERVES 8

4 slices white bread cubes, crusts removed, or
4 English muffins, cubed

$1/2$ cup (1 stick) butter, melted

3 large eggs, slightly beaten

1 cup sugar

2 tablespoons all-purpose flour

$1/8$ teaspoon salt

1 large can (20 ounces) crushed or cubed
pineapple, with juice

Lightly sweetened whipped cream, for serving

1. In a bowl, toss the bread cubes in the melted butter to coat, then set aside. In a large mixing bowl, combine the eggs, sugar, flour, salt, and pineapple with juice. Place in an 8- or 9-inch square glass baking dish. Top with the buttered bread cubes, cover, and refrigerate overnight.

The next day
2. Preheat the oven to 350°F. Bake the dessert until firm, about 30 minutes. This can be cut into squares or scooped into bowls and topped with lightly sweetened whipped cream.

Almond Featherbeds

The Huckleberry Inn
Warren, Connecticut
www.thehuckleberryinn.com

A guest called for a reservation, and during our conversation, he asked what we served for breakfast. I mentioned these Almond Featherbeds. He said, "That sounds very comfortable, but what do you serve for breakfast?" I explained that Almond Featherbeds were made from bread, not a type of bed covering. After much laughter, we promised to make these during his stay.—C.G.

SERVES 6

Butter, for greasing the dish(es)
4 cups challah bread, torn into 1- to 2-inch pieces
1 cup almond paste
1 cup mascarpone cheese

FOR THE CUSTARD
5 large eggs
1 1/2 cups whole milk
1/4 cup Amaretto liqueur
1/2 teaspoon salt

FOR THE CINNAMON SYRUP
1/4 cup (1/2 stick) butter, melted
2 teaspoons ground cinnamon

FOR ASSEMBLY
1/2 cup slivered almonds
Confectioners' sugar

1. Butter six 1-cup ramekins or an 8 × 8-inch ceramic baking dish. In the dish(es), arrange alternating layers of bread, almond paste, and mascarpone (use a teaspoon to add the paste and the cheese in small ¹/₂-teaspoon pieces).

2. Whisk the custard ingredients together in a bowl and pour over the bread mixture.

3. For the cinnamon syrup, combine the melted butter and cinnamon in a small saucepan. Gently warm. Drizzle the cinnamon syrup over the top, cover with plastic wrap, and refrigerate overnight.

The next day

4. Preheat the oven to 350°F. Uncover the featherbeds and sprinkle with the slivered almonds. Bake until puffed, golden brown, and set in the middle. (The baking time depends on the size of the dishes: about 25 minutes for ramekins, 45 minutes for an 8-inch-square pan.) Dust with confectioners' sugar and serve.

Pumpkin Pie Pudding

Ivy House Inn Bed & Breakfast
Casper, Wyoming
www.ivyhouseinn.com

This is a great fall morning wake-up or dessert.
The smell of cinnamon and pumpkin permeating
the bed-and-breakfast makes people very
happy and hungry. I like to serve this with slices
of ham, fresh apples (a caramel dip on the
side is nice), and whole-grain toast.
—TOM & KATHY JOHNSON, INNKEEPERS

SERVES 6 TO 8

Nonstick vegetable oil spray

1 can (15 ounces) pumpkin purée

1 can (12 ounces) evaporated milk

³/₄ cup brown sugar

¹/₂ cup Bisquick

2 large eggs, beaten

2 tablespoons (¹/₄ stick) butter, melted

2¹/₂ teaspoons pumpkin pie spice or 1¹/₂ teaspoons
ground cinnamon

¹/₂ teaspoon ground cloves

¹/₂ teaspoon ground ginger

2 teaspoons pure vanilla extract

¹/₂ cup chopped walnuts (optional)

Heavy cream or lightly sweetened whipped
cream, for serving

1. Coat the inside of a slow cooker with nonstick vegetable oil spray. In a large mixing bowl, combine all the in-

gredients except the heavy cream or whipped cream. Pour into the slow cooker, cover, and cook on the lowest setting overnight (up to 8 hours), or until the pudding reaches a temperature of 160°F.

The next day

2. Serve in bowls with heavy cream or whipped cream.

Buster Bar Dessert

Nantucket House of Chatham Bed & Breakfast
South Chatham, Massachusetts
www.chathaminn.com

This recipe is great for children's parties! You can have a lot of fun with this recipe. Use a sorbet between the ice cream layers. Be sure to freeze between the layers if you create more than one layer. Substitute chocolate jimmies or crushed Heath bars for candy topping. Crushed candy cane is cute for the holidays. Other ice cream flavors work well with this—adults enjoy coffee ice cream. You can also use crushed chocolate graham crackers as the crumb mixture. Watching calories? Use Edy's low-fat ice cream.

SERVES 12

FOR THE CHOCOLATE SAUCE
2 cups confectioners' sugar
$1/2$ cup (1 stick) butter or margarine
$1^1/2$ cups evaporated milk
$2/3$ cup chocolate chips

FOR THE ICE-CREAM-COOKIE CRUST
1 pound Oreo cookies, crushed
1/2 cup (1 stick) butter or margarine, melted
1/2 gallon vanilla ice cream, softened

FOR THE TOPPING
8 ounces whipped topping
Salted peanuts, M&M's, Reese's Pieces
Chocolate sauce

1. For the chocolate sauce, combine the sauce ingredients in a medium saucepan. Place over medium heat and boil for 8 minutes. Remove from the heat and cool to room temperature.

2. For the ice-cream-cookie crust, combine the crushed cookies with the melted butter in a large bowl. Pat the crumb mixture into a 9 × 13-inch baking pan. Spread the softened ice cream over the cookie layer and freeze until firm. Spread the chocolate sauce over the firm ice cream and return to the freezer.

3. For the topping, spread the whipped topping over the dish. Sprinkle with peanuts, M&M's, or Reese's Pieces. Cover with plastic wrap and store in the freezer overnight.

The next day
4. Allow the dessert to sit at room temperature for about 15 minutes to thaw slightly. Cut into squares. If desired, drizzle chocolate sauce over the top before serving.

Brandy Cheesecake

The Carlisle House
Carlisle, Pennsylvania
www.thecarlislehouse.com

This recipe was adapted from a recipe printed
in the *Washington Post* several years ago.
Cheesecake has never been better! Be careful
not to overcook the cake. It is best checked
after 7 hours in the oven.

SERVES 10 TO 12

Nonstick vegetable oil spray
$^1/_2$ cup graham cracker or cookie crumbs
2 pounds cream cheese, at room temperature
1 cup sugar
2 tablespoons pure vanilla extract
$^1/_4$ cup brandy
5 large eggs

1. Before you go to bed, preheat the oven to 200°F. Spray
the inside of a 9-inch springform pan with nonstick spray
and dust the bottom and sides with the crumbs. Set aside.

2. In a large bowl, mix the cream cheese with the sugar
until smooth and soft, scraping the sides of the bowl and
the spoon as necessary. Mix in the vanilla, brandy, and eggs
until the batter is well blended. Pour into the prepared
pan and place in the middle of the oven. Go to bed. If possible, plan to check the cake after 7 or no longer than 8
hours in the oven.

The next day

3. The cake should appear set, the top will have barely colored, and the surface will be smooth. Remove to a rack and cool in the pan for an hour until the pan is cool enough to handle.

4. Cover with a sheet of plastic wrap or wax paper (greaseproof paper) and an inverted plate. Holding the plate tight to the pan, invert both. Remove the pan and re-frigerate the cake upside down for at least 1 hour. The cake can stay all day like this.

5. Invert a serving plate over the cheesecake and invert the whole thing. Remove the top plate and the paper, cover, and refrigerate.

Chocolate Chip
Oatmeal Cookies

Nantucket House of Chatham Bed & Breakfast
South Chatham, Massachusetts
www.chathaminn.com

This recipe makes deliciously warm
chocolaty cookies every time.

MAKES 36 COOKIES

1^3/$_4$ cups all-purpose flour

1^1/$_4$ cups old-fashioned rolled oats

1 teaspoon baking soda

1 teaspoon salt

1 cup (2 sticks) butter or margarine

^{3}/$_4$ cup packed brown sugar

^{3}/$_4$ cup granulated sugar

1 teaspoon pure vanilla extract

2 large eggs

2 cups (12 ounces) of your favorite chocolate
chips or a combination of chips

1 cup chopped walnuts or pecans

1. In a large bowl, combine the flour, oats, baking soda, and salt; set aside.

2. In the bowl of an electric mixer, beat together the butter, sugars, and vanilla. Add the eggs one at a time, beating well after each addition. Gradually beat in the flour mixture. Stir in the chocolate chips and nuts. The cookie mixture can then be stored in a tightly covered nonmetallic container and refrigerated overnight or up to 2 weeks.

When ready to bake

3. Simply scoop out the amount you desire and bake. You'll always have warm chocolaty cookies! Bake in a pre-heated 375°F oven for 8 to 10 minutes. For chewy cookies, do not overbake.

Coffeecake Cookies

Flowers and Thyme Bed & Breakfast
Lancaster, Pennsylvania
www.flowersandthyme.com

It was summer and the windows were open.
A couple arrived after being lost trying to find
our inn. They literally said they "followed
their noses" to our door!—C.G.

MAKES 48 COOKIES

FOR THE COOKIES
4 cups all-purpose flour
1 teaspoon salt
$^3/_4$ cup sugar
$^3/_4$ cup shortening
1 envelope active dry yeast
$^1/_4$ cup lukewarm water (105 to 110°F)
1 cup milk
2 large eggs, beaten
1 teaspoon ground cinnamon

FOR THE ICING
$^1/_4$ cup ($^1/_2$ stick) butter, at room temperature
$1^1/_2$ cups confectioners' sugar
$^1/_2$ teaspoon pure vanilla extract

1. To make the cookies, combine the flour, salt, and $^1/_4$
cup sugar in a large bowl. Using a pastry blender or two
knives, cut in the shortening and set aside.

2. In a small bowl, dissolve the yeast in the lukewarm water. Heat milk in a small pan until steaming, then remove from the heat and allow to cool. Add the cooled milk to the yeast mixture, then stir in the eggs. Add the liquid mixture to the dry ingredients and stir lightly until the flour is moist; do not knead. Refrigerate overnight.

The next day

3. Preheat the oven to 350°F. Divide the dough in half. Roll each half out to a 12 × 8-inch rectangle about $1/4$ inch thick. In a small bowl, combine the remaining $1/2$ cup sugar with the cinnamon. Sprinkle each rectangle with the mixture. Starting at the longer end, roll up and slice in $5/8$-inch slices. Place on a nonstick baking sheet and bake until light brown, about 10 minutes. Cool.

4. To make the icing, melt the butter in a small saucepan over low heat and cook until it begins to brown. Remove from the heat and mix with the confectioners' sugar and vanilla. Add enough hot water to make it spreadable. Spread the icing on the cooled cookies.

Clifford Tea Cookies

The West Highland Inn
Ogunquit, Maine
www.westhighlandinn.com

The tradition of high tea dates back to the late 1700s. In England at that time, there were two daily meals, breakfast and dinner. To quiet her hungry stomach, the Duchess of Bedford began serving afternoon tea to her friends. Other hostesses quickly copied her idea. Typical high teas include thin, crustless sandwiches, sometimes a pâté, fancy petite cakes, petite scones, and a pot of your favorite tea.

MAKES 24 COOKIES

1 cup (2 sticks) butter

2 cups firmly packed brown sugar

2 large eggs

$3^1/2$ cups all-purpose flour, plus additional for rolling the dough

1 teaspoon baking soda

$^1/2$ teaspoon salt

1 cup finely chopped walnuts

1. In a large bowl, cream together the butter and brown sugar. Add the eggs and stir in $3^1/2$ cups flour, the baking soda, salt, and walnuts; mix well. Cover the bowl with plastic wrap and refrigerate overnight or up to 2 weeks.

The next day

2. Preheat the oven to 375°F. On a lightly floured surface, roll the dough ¼ inch thick. Cut with a cookie cutter and bake until lightly golden, 5 to 7 minutes. Allow to cool, then store in an airtight container.

Chocolate Ladyfinger Cake

The Redstone Inn
Dubuque, Iowa
www.theredstoneinn.com

Are you ready to wow your dinner guests? This is truly one of the prettiest desserts ever.

SERVES 12

4 large eggs, separated

2 bars (8 ounces each) German sweet chocolate

2 teaspoons pure vanilla extract

1 carton (9 ounces) whipped topping

1 cup finely chopped English walnuts

3 packages (3.5 ounces each) ladyfingers

1 cup heavy cream, whipped until stiff,
or frozen whipped topping

1. Using an electric mixer in a mixing bowl, beat the egg yolks until they are lemon colored. In a separate bowl, beat the egg whites until stiff peaks form.

2. Break the chocolate bars into a microwave-safe bowl and melt in the microwave. Remove from the heat and briskly whisk the egg yolks and vanilla into the chocolate. Fold the chocolate mixture into the stiffly beaten egg whites. When the mixture is cool, fold in half of the whipped topping and then the walnuts.

3. Using a 9- or 10-inch springform pan, line the bottom and sides with ladyfingers, placing the rounded side against the sides of the pan. Pour half of the chocolate mixture into the pan. Add another layer of ladyfingers and the other half of the chocolate mixture.

4. Fold the whipped cream and the remaining whipped topping together and smooth onto the top of the cake. It will just fill to the top of the standing ladyfingers. Cover and refrigerate overnight.

The next day

5. Place the cake on a cake stand and remove the sides from the pan. The cake can be decorated by tying a pretty satin ribbon around it so it looks like the ribbon is holding the cake together.

Pineapple Banana Frozen Dessert

Ostrander's Bed & Breakfast
Canton, New York
www.ostranders.com

The bride's parents and wedding party were our guests. They told us a package would arrive by UPS. It arrived and we placed it in the guest house refrigerator as instructed. On the morning of the wedding, the father came rushing into the house for us to come quick and help him. The package had contained butterflies. He had opened the box to place them in individual envelopes to release as the bride and groom came out of the church. It seems that butterflies are dormant when cold and very active when they warm up. Our guest house looked like a butterfly house, with them flying everywhere. However, we did manage to catch them, place them in the envelopes, and deliver them to the church on time.

—RITA OSTRANDER, INNKEEPER

SERVES 6

2²/₃ cups (about 7 medium) mashed ripe bananas

1¹/₂ cups sugar

1 can (20 ounces) crushed pineapple, undrained

6 ounces frozen orange juice concentrate, thawed

Sliced oranges and strawberries, for garnish

1. In a large mixing bowl, combine the mashed bananas, sugar, pineapple, orange juice concentrate, and 3 cups water. Mix well.

2. Pour into a 9 × 9-inch square pan, cover, and freeze overnight.

The next day

3. Remove the pan from the freezer 20 minutes before serving. Spoon into stemmed dessert serving dishes and garnish with orange and strawberry slices.

Chocolate
Mousse Crown

Nantucket House of Chatham Bed & Breakfast
South Chatham, Massachusetts
www.chathaminn.com

This is a dessert fit for a king or a queen!

SERVES 10

²/₃ cup coffee liqueur

2 envelopes unflavored gelatin

1 package (12 ounces) semisweet chocolate chips

3 eggs, separated

¹/₄ cup sugar

2 cups heavy cream, whipped until stiff

2 boxes Pepperidge Farm chocolate-filled
pirouette cookies

Whipped cream and shaved chocolate, for garnish

1. Place ¹/₂ cup cold water and the coffee liqueur in a saucepan. Sprinkle with the gelatin and let sit for 1 minute. Place over low heat and stir until the gelatin is dissolved, about 3 minutes. Gradually add the chocolate chips and stir until the chocolate is melted and smooth. Remove from the heat. Whisk in the egg yolks, one at a time. Cool to room temperature.

2. Beat the egg whites in a large bowl until stiff peaks form. Gradually add the sugar and beat until stiff glossy peaks form. Add a large dollop of the whites to the chocolate mixture and fold in. Fold the chocolate mixture into the remaining whites. Fold in the whipped cream. Spread 1 inch of the mousse in the bottom of a 9-inch springform pan. Line the rim of the pan with the cookies, breaking them in half so they come to slightly above the rim of the pan and pushing them into the mousse. Fill with the remaining mousse. Cover with wax paper and refrigerate overnight.

The next day

3. Remove the mousse from the springform pan. If desired, garnish with whipped cream and shaved chocolate.

Pear Strata

First Colony Inn
Nags Head, North Carolina
www.firstcolonyinn.com

This recipe is best served warm, not reheated, and does not keep for more than one serving. Substitute banana slices, canned or stewed apple slices, or pineapple tidbits for the pears.

SERVES 10 TO 12

Nonstick vegetable oil spray
6 thin slices day-old firm white bread, or as needed
2 cups whole milk
4 large eggs, lightly beaten

$^1/_2$ cup packed brown sugar

1 teaspoon vanilla extract

$^1/_4$ teaspoon salt

1 large can (29 ounces) pear halves or slices,
drained and rinsed

$^1/_2$ teaspoon ground cinnamon

1 cup low-fat granola (without raisins)

1. Spray an 8 × 8-inch shallow baking dish with nonstick spray. Place a single layer of bread in the dish.

2. In a large bowl, combine the milk, eggs, brown sugar, vanilla, and salt. Mix well, and pour over the bread. Chop or slice the pears thinly and arrange on the bread. Sprinkle with the cinnamon. Cover and refrigerate overnight.

The next day

3. Preheat the oven to 350°F. Sprinkle the granola over the pears. Bake until a knife inserted in the center comes out clean, 40 to 50 minutes.

Margaret Mosca's Zuppa Inglese
(Italian Rum Cake)

Nantucket House of Chatham Bed & Breakfast
South Chatham, Massachusetts
www.chathaminn.com

No matter what language you speak, your taste
buds will thank you for this fabulous dessert.
Serve it for a special occasion or as a
wonderful birthday treat.

SERVES 6 TO 8

FOR THE CAKE

Vegetable oil or nonstick vegetable oil spray

5 large eggs, separated

Finely grated zest of $1/2$ lemon

$1^1/2$ tablespoons lemon juice

$1^1/2$ cups sugar

1 cup sifted all-purpose flour

$1/4$ teaspoon salt

FOR THE CUSTARD FILLING

2 tablespoons ($1/4$ stick) butter

$1/4$ cup cornstarch

$3/4$ cup sugar

$1/2$ teaspoon salt

2 cups milk

2 egg yolks, slightly beaten

1 teaspoon pure vanilla extract
2 squares (1 ounce each) semisweet chocolate, melted

FOR ASSEMBLY
Dark rum
Sliced fruit or preserves
Lightly sweetened whipped cream

1. To make the cake, preheat the oven to 350°F. Oil or spray a 10 × 15-inch glass pan and set aside. In a mixing bowl, beat the egg yolks, gradually adding the lemon zest, lemon juice, and ¹/₂ cup of sugar. Mix together the flour and salt in a small bowl and fold into the egg yolks ¹/₄ cup at a time until it is all folded in.

2. In a separate bowl, beat the egg whites until foamy. Gradually add ¹/₂ cup of sugar and beat until stiff. Add the egg whites to the egg yolk mixture and gently fold together.

3. Spread in the pan and bake until the top is golden and springs back to a gentle touch, about 15 minutes. Allow to cool in the pan and cut into quarters; these will be stacked to make the layers of the cake.

4. To make the custard filling, melt the butter in a saucepan over low heat and blend in the cornstarch, sugar, and salt. Gradually add the milk until blended. Stir in the egg yolks and vanilla and cook, stirring constantly, until thickened, 2 to 5 minutes. Divide in half and add the chocolate to one half.

5. To assemble the cake, place one-quarter of the sponge cake on a serving tray and sprinkle with rum. Spread the

sponge cake with the chocolate custard and sprinkle liberally with rum. Add a layer of sponge cake, place sliced
fruit or preserves over the layer, and douse with rum.
Add another layer of sponge cake and sprinkle with rum;
spread with the plain custard and sprinkle again with
rum. Top with the last layer of cake and sprinkle with
rum. Cover with plastic wrap and refrigerate overnight.

The next day

6. Cover with whipped cream. If soupy, eat with a
spoon.

Strawberry and Chocolate Trifle

Brewster Teapot at the Beechcroft Inn
Brewster, Massachusetts
www.thebeechcroftinn.com

Trifles are wonderful because they look elegant and you can vary and have fun with the ingredients. They provide a nice accompaniment to the various delicious flavors of international teas.

SERVES 8

1¹/₂ pounds fresh strawberries, hulled and sliced

¹/₄ cup freshly squeezed orange juice

2 tablespoons orange liqueur, such as Cointreau or Grand Marnier (optional)

18 ounces mascarpone cheese

4 ounces light brown sugar

3 large eggs, separated

8 bar-sized chocolate brownies or chocolate cake slices, broken into small pieces

Lightly sweetened whipped cream, for garnish

2 ounces dark chocolate, grated or curled

1. In a medium mixing bowl, combine the strawberries, orange juice, and orange liqueur. Allow to stand for about 30 minutes.

2. In the bowl of an electric mixer, combine the mascarpone, sugar, and egg yolks and beat until smooth. In another large bowl, whisk the egg whites until they form soft peaks, then gently fold into the mascarpone mixture.

3. The trifle can be made in one large glass dish or in individual long-stemmed glasses. Tuck a good layer of the brownies in the bottom of a bowl or each glass. Add half the strawberry mixture and juices, then half the mascarpone mixture. Top with another layer of brownies, strawberries and juices, and finally, the remaining mascarpone. Cover with plastic wrap and refrigerate overnight.

The next day
4. Just before serving, top the trifle with a generous swirl of whipped cream and sprinkle with grated chocolate or chocolate curls.

Pumpkin
Bread Pudding

Harmony Hill Bed & Breakfast
Arlington, Virginia
www.harmony-hill.com

Pumpkins originated in Central America. The
largest pumpkin pie ever made was over five feet
in diameter and weighed over 350 pounds. It used
eighty pounds of cooked pumpkin, thirty-six
pounds of sugar, and twelve dozen eggs
and took six hours to bake.

SERVES 6

Vegetable oil or nonstick vegetable oil spray

1 tablespoon butter, softened

6 slices white bread, lightly toasted

$^1/_3$ cup raisins

$1^2/_3$ cups milk

1 cup fresh or canned puréed pumpkin

3 large eggs

$^1/_2$ cup brown sugar

1 teaspoon ground cinnamon

$^1/_2$ teaspoon freshly grated nutmeg

1. Oil or spray a 9 × 9-inch glass baking dish. Butter the toast and place in the dish, slightly overlapping the toast slices. Sprinkle the raisins on top.

2. In a large bowl, combine the milk, pumpkin, eggs,

brown sugar, cinnamon, and nutmeg. Mix well and pour over the bread. Cover and refrigerate overnight.

The next day

3. Preheat the oven to 350°F. Bake, uncovered, until a knife inserted near the center comes out clean, 35 to 40 minutes. Serve warm or cold.

Piña Colada Tiramisù

Nantucket House of Chatham & Breakfast
South Chatham, Massachusetts
www.chathaminn.com

If you like piña coladas, but can't escape to a warm sunny climate, close your eyes, play some Jimmy Buffett, and enjoy this fabulous dessert.

SERVES 12

2 packages (8 ounces each) cream cheese,
at room temperature

$^1/_2$ cup sour cream

1 can (21 ounces) Comstock pineapple pie filling

6 cups frozen whipped topping, thawed

3 packages (3.5 ounces each) ladyfingers

$^3/_4$ cup frozen piña colada mix, thawed

5 tablespoons coffee-flavored liqueur or cold
strong brewed coffee

$^2/_3$ cup toasted coconut

1. In a large bowl, beat the cream cheese until smooth. Add the sour cream and pie filling and beat again until well combined. Gently fold in 3 cups of the whipped topping. Separate the ladyfingers into halves.

2. In a wide shallow bowl, combine the piña colada mix with the liqueur or coffee. Dip half the ladyfingers quickly into the piña colada mixture and arrange over the bottom of a 9 × 13-inch glass baking dish. Spread half the cream cheese mixture over the ladyfingers. Dip the remaining ladyfingers in the piña colada mixture and arrange over the top of the cream cheese mixture.

3. Drizzle any remaining piña colada mixture over the second layer of ladyfingers. Top with the remaining cream cheese mixture, followed by the remaining 3 cups of whipped topping. Cover loosely and refrigerate overnight.

The next day

4. Before serving, sprinkle with the toasted coconut. Cut into squares to serve.

Easy Puff Pastry

Grant Corner Inn
Santa Fe, New Mexico
www.grantcornerinn.com

Every April Fools' Day, we try to surprise our guests by serving something outlandish and experiencing their reactions. Here's one: Serves 1—April Fools' Breakfast: Place two raw eggs on platter with two slices of raw bacon and decorate with an attractive garnish. Present the platter with a sweet smile and wait as long as possible for a reaction. Cook's memory: One of my most interesting reactions was, "But I didn't order meat!"

This recipe, one you'll use often, guarantees a positive reaction every time. Remember to keep the dough chilled; if it warms up as you work it, refrigerate for 30 minutes, then try again.
—LOUISE STEWART, INNKEEPER

MAKES 1 POUND

1 1/2 cups all-purpose flour
1 cup (2 sticks) well-chilled butter
1/2 cup sour cream
1/4 teaspoon lemon juice

1. Place the flour in a medium mixing bowl. Cut the butter into 1/2-inch cubes. Using a pastry blender, cut the butter into the flour until the mixture looks like coarse meal. Stir in the sour cream and lemon juice. Knead in bowl just until dough holds together in ball.

2. Flatten the dough into a rough 5 × 7-inch rectangle. Wrap in wax paper, then in plastic wrap. Chill overnight.

The next day
3. Let stand at room temperature 15 minutes before working with the dough, then work quickly!

Variations
You may wish to top the puff pastry with fresh fruits. Or you can try the following:

6 large cookies, crumbled
16 medium fresh strawberries, washed, hulled, and dried
2 teaspoons jelly
¼ cup sugar
1 egg beaten with 1 teaspoon water for glaze

Form the pastry into two disks. Sprinkle one with cookie crumbs, place berries on the crumbs, then dot with jelly. Sprinkle with sugar and brush with the egg glaze. Cut a 1-inch hole in the center of the second circle and set the pastry disk on top of the berries. Seal the edges together by crimping all around with the tines of a fork. Brush the top with the egg glaze and sprinkle with 1 tablespoon sugar. Chill 20 minutes. Bake at 450°F for 10 minutes, then reduce the heat to 400°F and bake another 20 to 25 minutes.

Frothy Strawberry Squares

Nantucket House of Chatham Bed & Breakfast
South Chatham, Massachusetts
www.chathaminn.com

If using frozen strawberries, partially thaw and reduce the sugar to ²/₃ cup. These are pretty for
Valentine's Day or a spring gathering.

SERVES 8 TO 10

1 cup all-purpose flour

¹/₄ cup brown sugar

¹/₂ cup chopped walnuts

¹/₂ cup (1 stick) butter or margarine, melted

2 large egg whites

1 cup granulated sugar

2 cups sliced fresh strawberries or 10 ounces frozen
strawberries, partially thawed

2 teaspoons lemon juice

1 cup heavy cream, whipped until stiff

Whole fresh strawberries, for garnish

1. Preheat the oven to 350°F. In a large bowl, combine
the flour, brown sugar, walnuts, and butter; mix well.
Spread evenly in a shallow pan and bake for 20 minutes,
stirring occasionally. Sprinkle two-thirds of this mixture in
a 13 × 9-inch baking dish.

2. In the bowl of an electric mixer, combine the egg
whites, granulated sugar, strawberries, and lemon juice.

Beat at high speed to stiff peaks, approximately 20 minutes. Fold in the whipped cream. Spoon the mixture on the crumbs in the baking dish and top with the remaining crumbs. Freeze overnight.

The next day

3. Cut into 10 or 12 squares and garnish with whole strawberries.

Index

crab dip, hot, 5–6
crabmeat canapés, 2–3
cranberry
    apricot risotto, 130–31
    nut breakfast rolls, 81–83
crawfish maquechoux, 204–6
cream biscuits, 192
crème brûlée French toast,
    46–47
crepes
    black raspberry, 244–46
    savory spinach, 196–99
croissants à l'orange, 56–57
crumb cake, blueberry, 125–26
custard filling, 271–73

decadent French toast soufflé,
    91–92
dips
    artichoke spinach, 10–11
    hot crab, 5–6
    six-layer, Nantucket House,
    16–17

easy puff pastry, 279–80
easy wild rice quiche, 120–21
eggplant
    mozzarella, 208–9
    Parma style, 190–91
eggs
    artichoke and roasted pepper
    soufflé, 217–18
    and bacon lasagne, 128–29
    Bayou Bend casserole, 43–44
    Benedict, 118–19
    blintz soufflé, 126–27
    breakfast pizza, 50–51
    Celebrations Inn veggie
    casserole, 123–24
    chili cheese puff, 19–20
    decadent French toast soufflé,
    91–92
    Ellie's Sunday strata, 58–59
    guten morgen, 42–43
    hard-boiled, 98
    Hattie's, 114
    potato Florentine casserole,
    206–7
    raw, xiv

    room temperature, for soufflés,
    126
    sausage puff, 24–25
    smoked salmon or Brie herb
    cheese puff, 14–15
    Southwestern, 71–72
    Southwestern frittata, 162–63
    Southwest strata, 37–38
    Spanish omelette, 154–55
    stuffed, casserole, 98–99
    Sunday breakfast casserole,
    48–49
Ellie's Sunday strata, 58–59

featherbeds, almond, 251–52
fillet of sole stuffed with shrimp,
    227–28
First Colony juice cordial, 61–62
First Lady's cheese spread, 26–27
Florentine casserole, 96–97
    potato egg, 206–7
French toast
    baked blueberry, 35–36
    bananas Foster, 40–41
    blueberry-stuffed, 45–46
    crème brûlée, 46–47
    decadent soufflé, 91–92
    Miller House Grand Marnier,
    116–17
    pineapple, with ambrosia salsa,
    134–35
    praline French bake, 67–68
    spiced pear, 100–101
    upside-down, Nantucket
    House, 63–64
frittata, Southwestern, 162–63
frothy strawberry squares,
    281–82
fruit
    hot casserole, 111
    salsa, Watch Hill Brie strata
    with, 94–95
    see also specific fruits

garlic bread, 153
German apple cake (apfelkuchen),
    242–43
Gordon family stuffed shells,
    188–89